Y0-CPC-470

250
V969 Voss, C.H.
c. 1

In search of meaning

DEC 15 '82	DATE DUE		
OCT 22 '88			

IN SEARCH OF MEANING:

Living Religions of the World

IN SEARCH

Illustrated by Eric Carle

THE WORLD PUBLISHING COMPANY

290
VOS

OF MEANING:

Living Religions of the World

CARL HERMANN VOSS

Excalibur Books

CLEVELAND AND NEW YORK

FLORA PUBLIC LIBRARY
Madison County Library System

Published by The World Publishing Company
2231 West 110th Street, Cleveland, Ohio 44102
Published simultaneously in Canada by
Nelson, Foster & Scott Ltd.
Library of Congress catalog card number: 67–23356
Text copyright © 1968 by Carl Hermann Voss
Illustrations copyright © 1968 by Eric Carle
WP
All rights reserved. No part of this book may be reproduced
in any form without written permission from the publisher, except for
brief passages included in a review appearing in a newspaper
or magazine. Printed in the United States of America.

Designed by Jack Jaget

To our daughter

CHRISTINE ELISABETH GIERLOTKA

and her generation

*Many roads hast Thou fashioned:
all of them lead to the light.*

—KIPLING

Contents

CONTENTS

EXCALIBUR BOOKS

Named after the legendary sword of King Arthur, Excalibur Books tell of courage, strength, and idealism. In a time when expediency, indecision, and cynicism so often seem to prevail, these books offer a creative alternative: they focus on persons of character, movements of historic significance, and beliefs of enduring value. They evaluate the past to appreciate and absorb its rich legacies, appraise the present, and seek meaning amid so much that appears to be meaningless.

Edited by Carl Hermann Voss, Excalibur Books cover a wide range of subject matter and interpret significant issues with candor and realism, imagination and sensitivity. The authors—each a leading authority in his field—explore the origin and meaning of established faiths. At the same time they venture beyond the framework of organized religion to examine the faith and deeds of secular idealists and to assay the interrelation of science and religion.

Excalibur Books have the primary purpose of making the resources of religion meaningful and relevant to young people in a changing world.

INTRODUCTION

Across a Void of Mystery and Dread

LONG BEFORE sagas of ancient tribes were recorded, re-ligions arose all over the world. Wise men and poets, seers and soothsayers, medicine men and dispensers of magic, chieftains and kings sought answers to perplexing questions. They tried to solve the mysteries of life and death. The religious rites and beliefs they created reflected a desire for knowledge about their own origin and their destination. The ancient peoples yearned for assurance that life had purpose and that death was not the end. As they confronted human existence they experienced awe, some-times fear, often exultation.

This was the beginning of religion: the efforts men made to accept and to adapt themselves to the world about them. Their environment was, for the most part, puzzling and unpredictable, hostile and at times destructive. Yet it might be full of beauty and joy; it might bring a measure of comfort and, in certain seasons and places, an amazing abundance. Life could be cruel and hard and was apparently meant to be brief; but above all else it was uncertain. Man could not control the elements of sea and sky, forest and field. He might kill wild beasts, catch huge fish, vanquish old enemies, conquer a nearby tribe; but in the world about him and in the life he so precariously lived, disasters came swiftly, without warning. Forces and powers over which he had no sway triumphed and seemed always to be ultimately victorious.

Primitive man thought that by observing a fetish—performing some ritual or allowing a medicine man, the *shaman,* to intercede for him—he might propitiate the hostile spirits. By offering thanks to benevolent spirits he might encourage them to grant more favors. The earliest among primitive men seem to have believed in spirits that were either hostile or neutral; later there developed a belief in forces that were benevolent and brought good, and men then began to hint at the idea of gods. At the same time, primitive men resorted to the device of hiding from what they considered to be evil forces or spirits.

In our day we may feel we have progressed far beyond primitive beliefs; in reality the customs and outlooks that mold our practices often originated in times before recorded history. There is, however, a difference between then and now: we look upon religion as the conduct which indicates our belief in, our reverence for, and our desire to please some divine power. By rites and observances we accord recognition to a higher power which has control of our destiny and to which we owe reverence and obedience. We construe religion to be the general moral and mental attitude which results from such beliefs and which affects both the individual and the community. We interpret religion as the forms of faith and worship which urge devotion to a principle or an idea that seems most worthy and demands a measure of fidelity to an ideal; we approve of such feelings and attitudes as standards for either a person or an entire nation in the practical struggle for survival.

These conceptions of religion in our own era differ to a great extent from the religious views and practices of long ago, some of which we now examine.

Foremost among the regions from which the earliest religions appear to have emerged was the Fertile Crescent, the semicircular area of cultivable soil which stretches northwest from the Persian Gulf, around the valley of the Tigris and Euphrates rivers, then southwest down along the Levant into Syria, Lebanon, Jordan, Israel, and the Nile valley of Egypt. Between the Tigris and Euphrates several important groups lived in antiquity: the Sumerians, the Babylonians, the Hittites, and the Assyrians. In their earliest centuries these peoples had been nomads, rovers believing in a number of gods, some of whom were thought to demand not only the first fruits of the herds and flocks but also the sacrifice of human beings. The devotees of these early religions glimpsed only dimly the ideas of good versus evil, of justice in contrast to inequity and exploitation. Such ideas were secondary to the immediate purpose of their religious rites: to stave off hostile spirits and to gain favor from friendly gods. They adhered to the *lex talionis,* the retribution law which allowed "an eye for an eye and a tooth for a tooth."

Among these peoples of the Fertile Crescent in the second and first millennia B.C., the Babylonians were perhaps the most enterprising and creative, drawing on the heritage left them by their Sumerian predecessors and making contributions to many cultures and in several significant areas of thought. Famed in part for the magnificence of their temples and tombs and the vast amount of their religious literature, the Babylonians are also remembered for their ethical standards. Centuries before the Israelites, Babylonian writings contained their own vivid versions of the creation, a flood, the expulsion of Satan from heaven and his descent into hell. The Code of King Hammurabi (1728–1686 B.C.) was unique in its comprehensive nature and its establishment of laws on a high level of justice and ethics. On the whole, the Code was humanitarian and protected the weak, the helpless, and the less fortunate.

The Assyrians (named after their chief god, Assur) never attained the higher ethics of the Babylonians; nor did they desire to do so. They seem to have been a fierce people who excelled in cruelty and savagery. Few ancient tribes could equal their bestiality; to them war gods were an absolute essential. Their religion affirmed no belief in a judgment after death and had therefore little influence on a man's conduct, certainly none to render him more humane and kind.

In contrast to the Babylonians and the Assyrians, the Hittites are far more obscure in history. It is known that they flourished from the twentieth century B.C. to about the thirteenth. In recent decades archaeologists have unearthed enough evidence to show that this once powerful nation, a potent cultural force in Western Asia, had an eclectic religion wherein beliefs of many kinds and from differing backgrounds prevailed; many gods were adopted from Babylonian and Assyrian patterns of culture.

To the south and west of the Tigris and Euphrates region lay the land of Egypt, revealing to the world an odd admixture of the worship of sun and nature, of animals and ancestors, along with what may have been a rather advanced form of belief in a godhead. In its earlier history of the third millennium B.C., Egypt was an isolated, self-sufficient, completely self-contained country; it had not only two major sectors—the kingdom of the Nile Delta, Lower Egypt, and the kingdom of Upper Egypt, extending to the First Cataract—but it was split up into "nomes," that is, a large number of autonomous districts with their own governing units and gods, usually portrayed as animals, to guard and protect them. As the nomes merged and eventually formed the two kingdoms, these became antagonists with a rivalry that lasted for many centuries. Later they united to become a nation of great strength and considerable influence.

The Egyptians looked upon animals as possessing remarkable power and conveying wisdom, fertility, and strength to men. In time they were symbolized in human form with the heads of animals among whom the most memorable was the ram, Amon.

The ancient Egyptians worshiped the Nile River and the sun—Osiris, the god of the Nile, his sister and wife, Isis, their son Horus, the god of darkness, Set, and Re, the sun-god who had as his symbols the pyramid and the winged sun disk. Worship of Osiris encouraged the worship of ancestors, for in the popular legend Osiris was killed by the god of darkness, Set, and was subsequently resurrected by the love and the mourning of Isis; this drama highlighted the Egyptians' belief in immortality.

Kings, thought of as divinities, built pyramids of rare beauty and great size to entomb themselves. They left orders for their bodies to be mummified and supplied with food, weapons, and clothes. *The Book of the Dead,* with its formulas to bring the soul to Osiris' judgment hall, granted an ornate burial to both rich and poor, ruler and ruled. Osiris judged the soul by the morality of a man's life, a new interpretation that made religion more than mere ritual as it directed men's minds toward the just and the moral.

Into this complex of beliefs that existed in the early part of the fourteenth century B.C. came Amenhotep IV. He is known also as Ikhnaton ("Spirit of Aton" or "Profitable to Aton") and is remembered as a sensitive, gentle, but courageous ruler who put aside Amon and all other gods to make Aton, "sun" or "light," the All Father or omnipotent God:

> Thy dawning, O living Aton, is beautiful
> on the horizon. . . . O Beginning of
> Life, Thou art all, and Thy rays encompass
> all. . . . Thou art the Life of life;
> through Thee men live.

In this famous "sun hymn" was embodied the highest development of Egyptian religion.

Soon, however, Ikhnaton's reforms were revoked. Upon his death the priests of Amon quickly regained control and destroyed Ikhnaton's architecture, literature, and art. A reaction set in. The eventual results were decay and corruption for the religion, the country, the land, and the people.

During the two millennia or more that these four peoples —the Babylonians, Assyrians, Hittites, and Egyptians— waxed and waned in their power and influence, developments in religion were under way in the Grecian peninsula and islands which would make themselves felt throughout the world down to this very day. Here men no longer groped blindly toward the light; they began to be illumined by it. The ancient Greeks refined beliefs and rites in the centuries from about 1,000 B.C. to almost the beginnings of the Christian Era and with their signal contributions in thought and conduct had an incalculable effect on the Western world.

When the Indo-Europeans poured down from Central Europe to fuse their destiny with the Minoan and Aegean civilizations around 2,000 B.C., they helped to create a host of native deities. The Indo-Europeans, of obscure origins, had practiced primitive forms of religion and had the usual array of gods and goddesses; these invaders from the northern regions brought to the superstitious people of the Greek plains and valleys a newer set of gods, some fresh terms to describe godly attributes and failings, and a hearty gusto in celebrating both the virtues and the vices of the gods and goddesses.

Confusion reigned. The Minoans and Aegeans had revered sea-gods and river-gods, fertility-gods and goddesses. Now there prevailed a bewildering complexity, a melange of old deities and new deities merging and then proliferating, vanishing and later re-emerging. More order and more unity began to develop, but pagan habits were hard to cure; polytheism and magic, recourse to superstitions and oracles were still strong and unrestrained.

All the gods resembled human beings. The only difference between gods and men lay in the superior strength and greater beauty of gods; these endowments entitled them to their immortality. Even here there was discrimination: only the most heroic of the men and the most favored among the gods were chosen for the Elysian fields, Greek mythology's paradise for the virtuous after their death; the vast majority of men, joined by some of the gods, went on to a spirit world which was dreary, dank, and dark. Life after death, it should be noted, did not assume as much importance among the Greeks as it had, for example, among the Egyptians.

During the long centuries that Greek mythology prevailed, Mount Olympus was the home of the gods; and in the pantheon of the Olympic gods, Zeus stood supreme as the father of all mankind. He was the god who reigned over humanity and, at the same time, over all the gods and goddesses, among whom were the twelve great gods: himself, Hera, Poseidon, Demeter, Apollo, Artemis, Ares, Aphrodite, Hermes, Athena, Hephaestus, and Hestias.

Zeus was not, however, the All Supreme, for he had to bow before destiny or fate. The gods might be suprahuman but they "lived and moved and had their being," just as did men, within the framework of history and of nature. Such forces as death and strife and terror, humor and error and folly, operated with Fate to spell men's—and the gods'—joy and woe, success or failure.

Religion in Greece took a new turn in the eighth and seventh centuries B.C. with the Athenian festivals and the mystery religions. In the mystery religions the Greeks sought personal salvation and the assurance of immortality by means of an emotional religion. The gods on Mount Olympus were remote, and the rites to honor and propitiate them, too formal and unemotional.

The most notable contribution of Grecian civilization, however, was that of the philosophers. Many of them were profoundly religious in their thinking as they sought a unifying principle behind all phenomena. As a study of ultimate reality and the causes and principles which underlie all thinking and all being, Greek philosophy differs from theology by ignoring dogma and by dealing with speculation, not faith. The pre-Socratics—venturesome thinkers like Thales, Anaximander, Heraclitus, Parmenides, Anaxagoras, and Democritus—tried to find the one natural element common to all being and all nature. Many of the more daring and courageous scorned the older, more conventional explanations of life and its origins; they scoffed at the gods and their frailties. Some endured expulsion from the city of Athens. The high-minded Socrates, though he stood in reverence before the gods, suffered death as his penalty for being both rational and skeptical.

Eventually, and almost inevitably, most of them (notable exceptions: Democritus and Protagoras) arrived at a belief in one God; Aristotle refers to Xenophanes as having been the first to believe in a unity of everything: "There is one God who is greatest among gods and men and is not like mortals either in form or in thought." Plato and Aristotle influenced religious thought profoundly through the next two and a half thousand years, Plato probably more so than his pupil, Aristotle: both emphasized the goodness and greatness of God. In spite of the philosophers, however, the popular religions continued with scarcely any change.

The persuasive power of works by such dramatists and poets as Aeschylus and Sophocles, Aristophanes and Pindar in the fifth century B.C. caused a literal, unthinking, uncritical belief in the gods to begin to give way. The effort of poets and philosophers to envisage a universe wherein the supreme problem was the moral struggle had a far-reaching effect. The Greek dramatists, focusing on good and evil, revenge and retribution, guilt and punishment, also upheld the objective of the good life: "Know thyself! Never exceed. The middle way is best."

In the closing years of the fourth century B.C., the Greeks in Asia Minor and, later, in Athens were attracted by the teaching of a philosopher named Epicurus. To him philosophy was more than its literal definition ("the love of wisdom"); it was the subordination of metaphysics to ethics so that pleasure might be the highest good. Although intent on making life happy, Epicurus did not counsel a careless indulgence: he advocated serenity and the avoidance of pain, intellectual rather than bodily pleasures, and a prudential social code of strict honesty and justice.

A more rigorous, somewhat sterner, but no less attractive school of philosophy was Stoicism. Led by Zeno of Citium and instructed by him in the *stoa poecile* ("the painted porch"), the young men of these same decades adhered to Zeno's interpretations of Socrates' ideals of self-sufficiency and virtue, Heraclitus' explanation of the physical universe, and Aristotle's logic.

After a century, Stoicism was introduced in Rome. In later decades, it included among its ardent adherents the scholar-emperor Marcus Aurelius, and the dramatist-philosopher-statesman Seneca. The Stoics' ethical creed, "to live consistently with nature," led them to subdue their passions, curb unjust thoughts, restrain all indulgence, and do their duty. Although mystery religions still attracted the Romans, many of them found Stoicism more in accord with their way of thinking and their mode of life. They preferred the Stoic outlook to any other school of Greek philosophy, for this approach to life, imported from Greece, had all the grace, logic, and power a vital religion was expected to give a man.

In their later centuries the religions of Greece and Rome were similar to each other and appeared to call for the worship of the same gods; but in the earlier period the religion of Rome was uniquely its own, quite different from that of the Greeks. The Greeks may have thought of their gods as persons, but Roman religious observances were much more animistic and were used to propitiate innumerable spirits for the purpose of safeguarding the worshipers' lives.

Primarily, the Romans concerned themselves with the

spirits of their houses and fields, their professions, ambitions, and ancestors. Holding these spirits in awe, they placated them with prayers and offerings. To them religion was like the fulfillment of a contract; the gods not only were to be appeased but even could be controlled by invoking the right words and using the proper rituals. To perpetuate his family the farmer gave offerings to his guardian spirit Genius for virility in men and to the goddess Juno for the power in women to conceive. To maintain his household's safety, the Roman worshiped Vesta, guardian spirit of the hearth fire; the *lares,* deified spirits of ancestors who watched over their descendants and guarded the fields; the *penates,* guardians of the entire household; and Janus, god of the beginnings and the guardian of the door.

Eventually a hierarchy of priests developed. The priests, looked upon as public officials, practiced divination, borrowing from the Babylonians the art—or the pretense— of determining the will of the gods by studying the constellations, observing flights of birds, and examining entrails of sacrificed animals. Often they were tempted to use their powers for purely political ends; public offices in Rome were secured as political spoils and civic morality was brought to a low level. These conditions Caesar Augustus tried to remedy without success.

In the Western hemisphere arose the religions of the Aztecs in Mexico, the Mayas in both Mexico and Central America, and the Incas on fertile plateaus high in the Andes Mountains of Bolivia and Peru. Although these religions are more recent (some of the rites developed to their highest forms in the twelfth to sixteenth centuries A.D.), the observances and beliefs have remained vague to us. Our ignorance about them is due partly to our inability to decipher their languages and read their writings, and partly to the

Portuguese and Spanish conquistadors of only four centuries ago, who thought they were serving their Christian God by effacing the remnants of written records and obliterating all traces of these well-developed religions.

Of these religions, that of the Aztecs seems to have been the most advanced. An elaborate priesthood in the temples conducted the rituals with rigor and regularity, performed the sacrifices, led the people in regular classes of instruction, interpreted the life-after-death concepts, held confessionals, and granted absolution. Despite rituals that were bloody and fertility ceremonies that were unrestrained, the Aztecs had a distinctive, highly developed religion of rare beauty and meaning. Its practices paralleled, in some instances, those of the Jewish and Christian religions: the monasteries and convents of the priests and priestesses, and the hymns so akin to the Psalms. Some of their leaders in later centuries held views which bordered on the belief in one God; in one place a temple was built to the "unknown god," not pictured in material or physical fashion and possessing spiritual attributes of a high level.

The Mayas, farther to the south, constructed a complex civilization graced with artistry, a unique development because such culture and beauty seldom flourished in the torrid zones. Many clues about Mayan religion survive, but specific information on names and meanings is lacking. Their gods were many and bizarre; their followers reflected awe before the mysterious, fear before the unpredictable and unknown. Lovely temples, daringly designed and tastefully executed, reflect a high level of aspiration and imagination among these Indians.

The religion of the Incas, parallel in many ways to those of the Aztecs and the Mayas, had elaborate ritual and complex organization, at the heart of which was the worship of *huacas* ("holy things"). In this state religion, the sun was the center of veneration; but above Ynti, the sun, was the higher god, Viracocha. Human sacrifice did not prevail as among the Aztecs, but it did exist.

Such were some of the precursors of today's prevailing religions, groping, sometimes feebly but often courageously, toward the light of reason and more creative "revelations." Still others might be mentioned, the religions of the Celts, the Slavs, and the Teutons, the Polynesians, the American Indians, and many another; each reveals faltering, often crude, yet noble and admirable attempts of the ancients to seek clues to the mystery of existence. Most of these faiths from long ago are now dead, but each in its era was a striking example of mankind's ceaseless search for meaning.

Nineteen centuries ago Plutarch, Greek essayist and biographer, ascribed to the goddess Athena the saying: "I am all that has been, is, and will be, and no mortal has yet lifted My veil." These words were inscribed by a priest to his deity Neith (whom the Hellenes identified with their Athena) on the wall of an ancient temple at Sais in the northwest delta of the Nile. Many years later, according to tradition, a pilgrim of another era visited the sacred site and wrote on the opposite wall: "Veil after veil have we lifted and ever the Face is more wonderful."

PART ONE

From the Far East

I
HINDUISM

The Vision Inward

WHEN MAHATMA GANDHI, the great nationalist leader of India in the twentieth century, urged his followers to "turn the spotlight inward," he was only emphasizing the essence of the Upanishads from at least twenty-five centuries earlier: "The senses turn outward. Man, therefore, looks towards what is outside and sees not the inward being. Rare is the wise man who . . . shuts his eyes to outward things and so beholds the glory of the *Atman* [the inner self or soul] within." Thus he interpreted afresh the insight which, in poetic form, served as a basic theme of the *Bhagavad-Gita* almost two thousand years ago:

Only that yogi
Whose joy is inward,

Inward his peace,
And his vision inward
Shall come to Brahman [the Ultimate Reality]
And know Nirvana [absorption in the One].

Such has always been the essential admonition of "Hinduism," the term used in the West to describe the religious beliefs and practices of 365 million Hindus, the majority of the people of India.

Hinduism had its origin in Hindustan, the immense region between the Narbada River and the Himalaya Mountains, and was named as such for the first time when Moslem invaders took a word from the Persian language to refer to the country of the Indus River. In former years "Brahmanism" was the term usually chosen to describe this religion; but Brahmanism is, in fact, only one of the historic periods of Hinduism.

Hinduism is indeed so vast and so complex a phenomenon that it cannot be defined with exactitude. It is a way of life, so all-embracing and all-absorbing that one Hindu writer, Govinda Das, has called it "an anthropological process" which assimilates ideas and customs from every era and every tribe it has encountered throughout its many centuries of history.

There are resources in Hinduism to meet many different needs—the devotional, the poetic, the ascetic, the sensual, the practical, the moral, the philosophical, and the material. Hinduism runs the entire gamut of existence. It includes primitive animism (the belief that natural phenomena and objects such as the wind, trees, rocks, etc. are alive and have souls, or are inhabited by demons and spirits) and is to be found in such elemental form among the simplest, poorest villagers of India numbering in the tens of millions. Hindu-

ism is, however, the religion also of such sophisticated intellectuals as the poet Rabindranath Tagore (1861–1941) or
India's former President, Sri Sarvepalli Radhakrishnan; for
such men, Hindus by birth, it has provided both spiritual
sustenance and intellectual nurture.

The development of Hinduism spans more than 3,500
years, from at least the fifteenth or sixteenth centuries B.C.,
when Indo-Europeans—"Aryans"—invaded India from the
northwest. Yet recent discoveries have dated what appear to
have been Aryan invasions as long ago as 5,000 B.C. In fact,
some archaeologists have deciphered ancient hieroglyphics
which indicate that many beliefs and practices unique to
India's religions—the ideas of karma and reincarnation, the
popularity of asceticism, methods of yoga, etc.—existed in
India long before the Aryan invasions and had emerged from
a complex, well-developed civilization of which we know
tantalizingly little.

It is apparent, however, that the Aryans brought their
own religion and soon merged these beliefs and customs with
those of pre-Aryan Indians. In centuries earlier than the
Aryans', India's religion seems to have been animistic; the
many local gods were appeased by offerings and were worshiped to assure abundant crops, long life, courage in battle,
and escape from danger. The Aryans, however, began to
create elaborate rituals and to write the Vedas—"Knowledge"—in the Sanskrit language. Their priests and scribes
gathered prayers and formulas for conduct; they collected
rituals and hymns dealing with some of the more important
gods, especially the Sun (Surya), Rain, and Earth, which
were designated by various names in different regions.

The oldest and most important of these sacred books of
India was the Rig-Veda, a collection of hundreds of hymns
and prayers to various gods: the mother-goddess (Prithivi-

Matar), the father-sky (Dyaus Pitar), the sun-god (Mitra), and such nature deities as the storm-god and war-god (Indra), the mountain-god (Rudra), the god of the skies (Varuna), the god of the dawn (Ushas), the god of fire (Agni), the god of the dead, of heaven and hell (Yama), and the spirit of the drink-god (Soma), the brew that strengthened Indra for incredible feats. Families of priests chosen for the vocation of priesthood composed prayers and hymns of the Rig-Veda in the tenth and ninth centuries B.C.

For these many gods there were no temples in the earliest period of the Vedic religion, based on the Aryans' sacred writings of the Vedas. Likewise there were no images of such gods. A priesthood had emerged from the older religion of the Aryans, and in Vedic days these priests offered sacrifices at seed time and harvest, the full moon and the changing of seasons, and made use of grain and cakes, dairy products and animals, among which the horse was the most valued.

The simple forms of worship in the Vedic days (from about 1,000 B.C. to about 500 B.C.) heartily and happily affirmed life. Religion encouraged men to increase their herds, to till the land for plentiful crops, and to seek an abundant prosperity. The people of those days believed in magic, as is reflected in the Atharva-Veda, a fascinating collection of incantations, charms, curses, and blessings for every grievance and emergency a man or woman might face, from agricultural problems to emotional ills.

Parallel to these developments was the growth of the castes. With each successive wave of invasion moving farther south into the Ganges delta, the Aryans subjugated the dark-skinned natives and made them the lowest class in the social order. They divided themselves into three upper classes: the Brahmans, or priests; the Kshatriyas, or warriors, among whom were the kings, nobles, and most government officials; and the Vaisyas, or artisans and peasants, men of mercantile status. A fourth caste with many gradations, the Sudras (the vanquished people), served these three higher castes and undertook all kinds of work considered too menial for the upper castes. Then, a fifth caste, the Pancamas (known also as Pariahs or Asprishyas, or "Untouchables"), had the most lowly of occupations; strictly speaking, however, the untouchables were really outside the caste system. The Brahmans, as the priests, used religious sanctions and superstitions in such a way as to monopolize certain priestly functions for themselves and rendered the caste system a virtually unbreakable pattern. Through the centuries castes have been malleable for almost imperceptible changes on intermediate levels, but the status of Brahmans and Untouchables remained unchanged.

In the sixth century B.C., the concepts basic to Hinduism as we know it came into being. A new, negative spirit appeared. The Vedic religion of the past gave way to an involved structure of reflection and rituals explained by the Brahmans in the Brahmanas and in the Upanishads. The former, the Brahmanas, contained details concerning sacrifices to the various gods and sought to discern an underlying unity amid the multiplicity of gods. The latter, the Upanishads, began to speculate in earnest about the world which the Vedas had not critically appraised.

According to Hinduism a man's life had four stages: the student, who concentrated on the Vedas for a number of years; the householder, who married, raised a family, and was a responsible citizen; the forest dweller or hermit, who gave up his home to meditate in isolation from life; and the ascetic, alone and aloof from all family life, who became a mendicant intent solely on meditation. The Brahmanas had supplementary material, "Forest Treaties" (Aranyakas), designed to supply material for the meditations of those in the third period; they also gathered additional books, the Upanishads, which ultimately were to develop into the basis for all modern Indian philosophy.

The old gods, so many and so varied, vanished. In their place stood Brahman, the World-Soul, who was the One, the Creator, the Self-Existent, the sum of all that was and is, the It, the That. Here was a dramatic change from the Vedic faith of former centuries which had upheld a joyous, fulfilling life. In this new period of the Upanishads, men were attracted by a pessimism, drawn by an urge to flee from life, reject its joys, renounce its comforts, and withdraw from the world. Only thus could a man become holy, seek to elicit reverence and merit respect. To this outlook on life only the Brahmans, and later the Kshatriyas, were attracted.

Hinduism now introduced the doctrine of a universal soul with which the individual soul could be reunited after he had overcome *maya,* the illusion of time and space. Only dimly had the Rig-Veda hinted at these two new ideas of *samsara,* a rebirth by the transmigration of souls or reincarnation, and *karma.* The thinkers of India considered themselves to be on a wheel of rebirth, whirling ceaselessly; to them religion's basic purpose was to learn how a man might find release from that wheel, freedom from the necessity of coming back to live on earth in an endless cycle of reincarnation.

Tied to this idea of rebirth was the law of karma, an Indian version of the belief common to every culture that "whatsoever a man soweth, that shall he also reap." In India this "law of the deed" kept men on the wheel of life and therefore the perplexing question arose: how could a man

overcome karma to be released from the wheel? The Upanishads—meaning "confidential sessions" or "intimate sit-
tings with a teacher," and often called the Vedanta, "conclusion of the Vedas"—focused now on something other
than the techniques of the sacrifices. The emphasis centered
instead on salvation through contemplation.

The goal was the union of the soul (Atman) with the
World-Soul (Brahman). But only through insight could
this be achieved. Knowledge derived from insight—the
illumination that came from contemplation—held the secret
for release from karma. If a man realized that life was sheer
illusion (i.e., maya), he would know suffering no more. If
he saw that nothing in life was real, that all was illusory, he
could escape and identify with the World-Soul, Brahman,
God.

The system of yoga arose from this desire to secure the
requisite knowledge to bring release. Yoga prescribed specific directions for meditation: suspend all physical functions, including breathing; suppress all mental activities until pure peace of mind and body are attained. It calls for both
physical and mental control, but it is not a denial of action;
action is to be performed without involvement or attachment.

The Vedic religion of many gods and involved rituals
merged with the Brahmanic religion of the priests and their
sacrifices to produce a philosophic Hinduism; but it, in turn,
created a trend toward virtual agnosticism, as in Jainism and
Buddhism. Both Jainism and Buddhism then flourished
from about 600/500 B.C. to about A.D. 400/500 and made
a frontal attack on the elaborate ideas and rituals of the
Hinduism of those ten to eleven centuries. The Brahmanism of the time, adopting some features of those religions,
created the *Laws of Manu,* a book of its own rituals. Hindu-

ism, biding its time, soon was absorbing its competitive religions in India. The major direction for those who still accepted Hinduism was belief in a supreme God, personal and all-encompassing. The end result was a newly founded Hindu trinity, the Trimurti, of Brahma, Creator and All-Father as a male manifestation of Brahman, "the Great All"; Vishnu, the Preserver; and Shiva, the Destroyer.

In the Rig-Veda, Vishnu had been inferior to Varuna, in earliest times the god of the sky, who, it might have been predicted, was to become a god of ethical power, perhaps even of supremacy; yet Varuna receded in importance until he was no more than a water-god. Vishnu became much more significant, especially in his various incarnations such as the Fish, the Tortoise, the Boar, the Man-Lion, Gautama Buddha, the Horse, etc.

Shiva was worshiped but was additionally honored because his wife was also the object of worship, especially in her 1,008 names; as Kali, most frightful and frightening, she called for bloody sacrifices.

After the reform movements of the Jainists and the Buddhists had emerged and slowly moved under way during the sixth century B.C., Hinduism began to encourage the use of images and the construction of temples. Now images abounded; temples were built in such numbers and to such an extent in the next fourteen centuries that India now has more images and temples than any other country in the world. A sacred city like Benares has the greatest number of temples in all India; and millions of pilgrims go there every year to bathe in the Ganges because they consider it to be holy and capable of bestowing special blessings upon them.

As Hinduism adapted itself to changed conditions in India during and after the sixth century B.C., it formulated four permissible goals in living and approved of three ways to salvation, all seven of which meant new directions for the pilgrims and devotees. Of the four goals in life, two went along the path of desire and two, the way of renunciation:

(1) The first was pleasure (*kama*), particularly through love, physical exercise, and intellectual pursuits. For the uninitiate, Vatsyayana's *Kamasutra* instructed in the art of love; and the *Natyasastras* provided a knowledge of drama, poetry, and storytelling. A man was to realize, however, that something more durable and satisfying lay beyond such pleasure seeking.

(2) The second goal was power and possessions (*artha*) which would lead to social standing and material success. *Artha,* signifying both wealth and influence and based upon relentless competition and an admitted quest for affluence, was not to be condemned; but the seeker would learn that *artha* was not a high objective. Ultimately it would give way to a third—and later a fourth—along the paths of renunciation.

(3) The religious and moral law, *dharma,* opened a more worthwhile and satisfying life, for the *dharma*-follower served family and caste, community, and country. Instructed by the *Laws of Manu* and the *Dharmasastras* (the law books), he could serve the good of everyone and forswear an ego-centered striving for social advancement and financial gain, for sensual joys and personal delights. Yet the great happiness he knew in his loyalty to a high ethic was only partial. There was really but one genuine satisfaction, *moksha,* which meant authentic liberation or salvation.

(4) *Moksha* was the highest goal, the Hindu ideal of final redemption; but it could be attained only by being released from the endless cycle of rebirths and all the problems of life.

Hinduism then pointed to the three ways of salvation:

the Way of Works (*Karma Marga*); the Way of Knowledge (*Jnana Marga*); and the Way of Devotion (*Bhakti Marga*).

(1) The Way of Works (*Karma Marga*), time-honored method of observing duties, especially within one's own caste as outlined in Hindu scriptures, was designed to earn merit for a man and, in accord with the law of karma, to guarantee to that individual who performed more good deeds than bad that he would have the highest form of reincarnation in the next life. The Way of Works required sacrifices and rites at all important stages of life from birth to death, and honor of the spirits of departed ones in the family.

(2) The Way of Knowledge (*Jnana Marga*) had its foundation in the thought of the Upanishads which taught that ignorance (*avidya*) caused all evil and misery. Right thinking and abolition of ignorance were the cures for mental mistakes and counterforces to wrongdoing. If a man knew Brahman, he had begun to understand and apprehend that which was "real," for only Brahman was true reality. If a man studied all of the sacred writings, practiced the disciplines of yoga, and meditated intensively on Brahman, he would be spared both "suffering and evil." If a man considered himself to be a separate self apart from the All-Soul and remained ignorant of Brahman, he was doomed to the unchanged, unchanging fate of the ceaseless cycle of the law of karma. Only lifelong, disciplined preparation could bring the knowledge, lightning-like within an instant of illumination, that salvation was at hand: the pilgrim along the Way of Knowledge would be conscious that the law of karma was no longer effective and his repeated rebirths were at an end.

It was at this point that the Way of Works and the Way of Knowledge merged for the observant Brahman, and the four stages (*ashramas*) could become goals to be sought: as the student of religion, as the married man and householder, as the hermit or recluse, and as the holy man-mendicant.

(3) The Way of Devotion (*Bhakti Marga*) filled a need which could not be met by the Way of Works, so practical and so legalistic, or by the Way of Knowledge, so philosophical and so intellectual. The Brahmans realized that the common people were unmoved by the intellectualism of the higher classes but were attracted, especially in later centuries, by temple worship and by temple priests, as well as by piety in their private lives. The common man's awe before unseen powers and unknown mysteries led him to *bhakti,* the dependence on an impassioned worship of deities, both gods and goddesses. *Bhakti* did not deny the worth of the Way of Works or the Way of Knowledge; on the contrary, those two ways were heightened in their importance. The Way of Devotion contended, however, that it was only one of the real ways, true and tested, to achieve salvation, not distinct from the other two Ways, but perhaps in conjunction with them.

From the growing popularity and seeming efficacy of the Way of Devotion (*Bhatki Marga*) as a means to assured salvation came the great religious classic *Bhagavad-Gita* ("Song of the Blessed Lord"). It told of the Kshatriyas, but in particular of the god-hero Krishna, as he led the Pandavas in their successful war against their blood relations, the Kaurava princes (the War of the Bharats three thousand years ago). The great Pandava warrior Arjuna must lead his brothers and their fellow soldiers against his cousins, the princes of the Kaurava clans; but he hesitates. The call to battle brings both sides into furious, thunderous combat, but still Arjuna falters, confessing to Krishna his horror at the internecine strife and the senseless slaughter. Not so, says Krishna; and in a long discourse urges Arjuna to the battle, justifying its purpose and its carnage in terms of the promised salvation through higher knowledge, good works, and unselfish devotion. Krishna then reveals himself as Vishnu, the Preserver god, the Eternal Brahman. Arjuna is almost overcome at the supernal sight. At Arjuna's pleading that he resume human form, for the vision has been too dazzling and awesome, Vishnu becomes the charioteer, Krishna, again. But Krishna's point is clear: unconditional surrender in devotion, the unreserved *bhakti,* is the message of the "Song of the Blessed Lord." Its influence on Hinduism was so profound that about A.D. 100 it was melded into the great epic of over 100,000 couplets, the saga of the Kshatriya caste, *Mahabharata;* and even today this unique poem, as a vivid, powerful part of the *Mahabharata,* has extraordinary prestige. It has satisfied the intellectual and the devotional needs of Hindus more than has any other writing in Hinduism, probably because it succeeded so well in interweaving the three Ways of release: Works, Knowledge, and Devotion, and perhaps because it so dramatically illustrates the meaning of the word "avatar." Just as Rama, the hero of the folk epic *Ramayana,* was an avatar or embodiment of Vishnu, so was Krishna.

The Way of Devotion demanded self-dedication in loving devotion to one or another god or goddess, for each reflected Brahman and tended to instill some specific aspect. A man might rid himself of evil and merit the reincarnation if he were devoted to the deities, especially the Preserver-god Vishnu and his helper-gods, or the Destroyer-god Shiva and his cohorts among the lesser gods. Vishnu, linked with Brahman and assuming a physical body by which he can overcome evil, is divinely reincarnated in the god Krishna who had urged his followers:

. . . Cling thou to Me!
Clasp Me with heart and mind! So shalt thou dwell
Surely with Me on high. But if thy thought
Droops from such height; if thou be'st weak to set
Body and soul upon Me constantly,
Despair not! Give Me lower services! Seek
To read Me, worshipping with steadfast will;
And, if thou canst not worship steadfastly,
Work for Me, toil in works, pleasing to Me!
For he that laboreth right for love of Me
Shall finally attain! But, if in this
Thy faint heart fails, bring Me thy failure! Find
Refuge in Me!

Shiva, the Destroyer, is a god who can control all the
destructive elements. He has help from other gods and goddesses when he creates earthquakes and floods, famines and
catastrophes; but Hindus believe that, as the Destroyer,
Shiva brings good too, for his destructive nature returns
things to Brahman. The deities around Shiva are many; but
outstanding is the goddess Kali, the "divine wife," who de-
vours human flesh and, also known as Durgas, is worshiped
by, among others, the caste of robbers known as Thugs.
    These three Ways led then to a fourth Way, the Way of
Concentration, which enabled an individual to be freed of
both conscious and unconscious thought, thus to uncover
the real self which is identical with the All-Soul, Brahman.
Only by strict and careful discipline of the self can this be
attained. The simple things come first: do not lie, do not
cheat, do not steal, remain controlled, stay clean, study
regularly. But one thing more is important, all important:
avoid distractions, sit in a cross-legged position like the lotus,
control the breath, and subdue all sensation. In that manner

a man can lose consciousness of both time and himself and be absorbed into Brahman.

Hindu priests may minister at the local shrines; but they are aided—and sometimes hindered too—by the *yogin,* the *swami,* and *guru.* The yogin or yogi renounces worldly life and, by methods of yoga, seeks to attain reunion with Brahman, as he extinguishes or "blows out" the flame of life. A swami receives this Hindu title of respect because, as a member of a religious order and as a religious teacher, he vows poverty, chastity, and obedience. A guru is a preceptor who gives general guidance on religious matters, while *upadya* and *acharya* are religious teachers entrusted with the task of teaching the Vedas, usually to boys and young men but often to entire families as well.

The yogis hope to reach the level of the *sannyasis* and the *sadhus.* The former, the sannyasis, are often devotees of Shiva and have taken vows of renunciation and have been true ascetics in their estimation, thus attaining the fourth stage of the cycle of life, the existence of a holy man. The sadhu ("one who has renounced") has reached the goal of spiritual unity with Brahman and has experienced *samadhi* (the ultimate trance); he is considered, therefore, genuinely holy. Sadhus are familiar to us in the West from pictures of holy men of Hinduism subjecting themselves to tortures of fire and, by self-mastery, overcoming pain and ignoring sensation.

The average man in India is polytheistic, because he reveres all supernatural beings; and of these there is no end. To the Hindu his deities number, as he often says, 330,-000,000 gods. He may worship in his own home or in a temple, at a family altar or before a sacred shrine in his locality; but he also feels impelled to visit the sacred places which abound in India—in many instances caves in the hills or huts along the roads, but for the most part the mighty rivers of the land. The Ganges—"Mother Ganga"—is the holiest river, noted for many sacred places throughout its length from source to mouth, but especially for three: Hardwar, Allahabad, and Benares. Hindu belief holds that if a person dies in Benares, he will achieve salvation, the heaven of never-ending delight, where Shiva resides.

The most baffling aspect of Hinduism, when judged by Westerners, is the veneration of the cow. Killing of cows is forbidden. Honoring cows with garlands to adorn their necks and oil to anoint their foreheads is considered the cow's due. Mahatma Gandhi defended "cow protection" as a "central fact of Hinduism, the one concrete belief common to all Hindus . . . one of the most wonderful phenomena in human evolution." He considered protection of the cow to signify "protection of the whole dumb creation of God." In almost all the small villages of India cow dung is used for purposes ranging from medicine and disinfectant to fuel, and it often serves as an ingredient in mixing plaster or mortar.

Oddly enough, alongside such features of Hinduism as its polytheism and holy men, its myriad sacred sites and holy rivers, and its cow worship, stand many more liberal features. Within Hinduism over the centuries there have been strong and effective reform movements. One of the most effective reformers was Sankara, who lived at the end of the eighth century and the beginning of the ninth century A.D. A philosopher and Vedanta commentator of astuteness and originality, he is revered to this day as one of India's greatest spiritual leaders. It was Sankara who composed one of the Hindus' favorite prayers:

O Lord, pardon my three sins:
I have in contemplation clothed in form Thee who art
   formless!
I have in praise described Thee who art ineffable!
And in visiting shrines I have ignored Thine
   omnipresence.

In similar fashion millions of Hindus utter each day the
anonymous prayer: "As different streams having different
sources and with wanderings crooked or straight, all reach
the sea, so, Lord, the different paths which men take,
guided by their different tendencies, all lead to Thee." If it
be objected that too many gods impede spiritual progress in
Hinduism and blind men to one God, remember India's
foremost philosopher, former President Sarvepalli Radhakrishnan, who said:

"Those who live in God do not care to define. They have
a peculiar confidence in the universe, a profound and peace-
ful acceptance of life in all its sides. Their response to Ultimate Reality is not capable of a clear-cut, easily intelligible
formulation. The mystery of God's being cannot be rationally determined. It remains outside the scope of logical concepts. Its form does not lie in the field of vision, none can
see it with the eye. There is no equal to it. An austere silence
is more adequate to the experience of God than elaborate
descriptions."

It is just such a spirit which enables Hindus to tolerate
the beliefs of others and to grant freedom of operation even
to religions remote from and alien to their own beliefs, a
tolerance and respect which stand in sharp contrast to their
own caste system, so rigid until this generation. An example
of this attitude is their respect for the ancient religion of
Zoroastrianism. Zoroastrianism was the faith adopted by the

Persian kings, who were called Achaemenidae; they made it
a state religion. Records are few and sparse, yet it is known
for certain that Cyrus the Great, king of Persia from about
550 B.C. to his death in 529, was at least a nominal Zoroastrian, and it is an established fact that Xerxes was a devout
Zoroastrian. Zoroastrianism would have become one of the
chief religions of the West if Xerxes' invasion of Greece had
succeeded; his defeat at Salamis in 480 B.C. turned the tide
against the widespread acceptance of his religion.

Zoroastrianism was all but abolished in the seventh and
eighth centuries, when Islam became the religion of Persia.
Small groups remained devoted to the teachings of Zoroaster, the founder of the religion. Some scholars maintain
that Zoroaster lived from 660 B.C. to 583 B.C., while others
contend that 570 B.C. to 500 B.C. are more accurate dates.
Many argue, with logic and conviction, that Zoroaster lived
several centuries earlier, perhaps before 1,000 B.C. After his
death he was virtually deified; myths about him grew to
vast proportions, and as in many other religions, hindsight
cast him in a supernal light. Zoroastrians today are a small
group, but their importance is disproportionately great. The
Parsees of modern Iran—about 12,000 in number—practice
Zoroastrianism, with fidelity and strict adherence to ancient
rites.

The Parsees of India—roughly 120,000 in number—live
near Bombay and are a prosperous group whose economic
power and influence in India are far-reaching, and whose
prestige is great due in large measure to the influence Zoroastrianism has had on Judaism, Christianity, and Islam.

Sometimes the tolerance of other religious groups shown
by the Hindus is mere indifference; but sometimes, on the
more intellectual levels, it has a tendency to adopt what is
best in that faith. This conviction caused the great reformer

of a century ago, Ramakrishna, to say: "Different creeds are but different paths to reach the Almighty. As with one gold various ornaments are made, having different forms and names, so one God is worshiped in different countries and ages, has different forms and names." Ramakrishna is remembered by India because he strengthened the self-assurance, dignity, and pride of Hindus in our times, influencing, most of all, Mahatma Gandhi. Both men were saintly, Gandhi less so perhaps because he led the Indians' decades-long political struggle for independence and freedom; but like Ramakrishna, he prayed that everyone "may develop to the fulness of his being in his own religion—that the Christian may become a better Christian and the Mohammedan a better Mohammedan."

Hinduism, which has worshiped God as Many, and as Three, and as One, had until recently been in decline over the past 1,000 years and more. It fostered superstition and resorted to magic. It sanctioned social injustice and encouraged an escape from this world.

Logically enough the younger generation seemed therefore to follow Pandit Nehru, the newly independent India's first prime minister, in saying that religion had brought only misery and slavery in the past and should be avoided in the future; Nehru appeared to sound the doom of Hinduism. But now the most flagrant among the corruptions of Hinduism—child marriage and the caste system, enforced widowhood and *suttee* (the self-cremation of a widow on the funeral pyre of her husband)—have been abolished. India as a nation has undergone vast changes and welcomes the inductive science of the West and the political institutions of Western lands.

Today Hinduism is faced by two major problems: the impact of secularism, as science and technology lead many to reject religion, considering Hinduism to be superstitious, pessimistic, and antiquated; and the breakup of the caste system, partly because in 1950 the Indian government abolished the status of the untouchable and forbade such discrimination, and partly because a modern industrial society makes the exclusiveness of the caste system impossible to maintain.

All this has greatly affected the Indians and gives promise of making for enormous changes in Hinduism in coming years. The drive for social reform will inevitably alter the face of India; and Hinduism will be altered, too, as it has often been through several millennia, but it will not vanish. Its resources, intellectual and spiritual, traditional and cultural, are too great.

II
JAINISM

The Three Jewels

N O PERSON can achieve salvation, say the teachings of Jainism, unless his life is enhanced by the Three Jewels: right faith, right knowledge, and right conduct. These are the true means of final liberation.

In the sixth century B.C., Jainism arose as a protest against what seemed to its followers to be the excesses of Hinduism. Objecting to the stifling impersonality and involved ritualism they found in Hinduism, the Jains challenged the accepted religion. They resisted the claims of the priestly caste, the Brahmans, that only a Brahman could master the stages culminating in nirvana; moreover, many among the Kshatriyas, the kings' and chieftains' caste, opposed the Brahmans' insistence that the physical world was unreal.

Amid such latent rebellion and resistance the founder of this faith, Mahavira, was born in the first year of the new century, 599 B.C. The son of a rajah, he was raised amid luxury and married a princess by whom he had a daughter.

At the age of thirty, he decided to give up his life as a prince and to become a religious ascetic; but this action he postponed until his parents had died. After his parents' death he secured his older brother's consent and then pre- pared to relinquish all his belongings—gold and silver, jewels and ornaments, troops and chariots. He plucked out his hair in five handfuls, as a symbol of self-renunciation, and vowed: "I shall for twelve years neglect my body and abandon the care of it." He swore to endure with equanim- ity any calamity which might come from divine powers, from animals, or from men. He set out alone, discarding his robe and wandering naked across the plains and into the villages of central India in search of release from the cycle of birth, death, and then rebirth.

The chronicles of his life described for future generations his disdain for both comforts and discomforts: "He was indifferent alike to the smell of filth and of sandalwood, to straw and to jewels, to dirt and to gold, to pleasure and to pain, attached neither to this world nor to that beyond, de- siring neither life nor death."

Mahavira, "The Venerable One," paid no heed to cold or heat, we are told, for he "desired nothing of the kind; strong in control, he suffered, despising all shelter." He re- fused to "sleep for the sake of pleasure; he waked up him- self, and slept only a little. Purgatives and emetics, anoint- ing of the body and bathing, shampooing, and cleansing of the teeth do not behoove him."

Two major convictions impelled him: a complete asceti- cism and an absolute pacifism. The two were as one, for the soul could not be saved from evil without practicing such intense self-denial; and the soul could not maintain its purity and integrity unless a man practiced *ahimsa*—that is, non-injury—to all living beings. ("Harmlessness," he was accustomed to say, "is the only religion.")

In the thirteenth year of his wandering as a naked ascetic, the traditions relate, Mahavira was "in a squatting position . . . exposing himself to the heat of the sun . . . with the knees high and the head low, in deep meditation, in the midst of abstract meditation, [when] he reached nirvana, the complete and full, the unobstructed, infinite Absolute."

Now that he had succeeded in gaining control over both the world and his own body, Mahavira gave up being a solitary bent on asceticism; he became instead a leader of men and the teacher of monks. Thereafter he was called "The Conqueror" (Jina). For the following thirty years, until he died at the age of seventy-two in 527 B.C., Mahavira preached and taught with extraordinary success.

His followers became known as Jains, disciples of him who conquered. Had he not conquered? Had he not attained victory over his own body and its desires?

Mahavira, a disillusioned nobleman of the warrior caste (the Kshatriyas) in Hinduism, had adopted the asceticism of the Parshva order of mendicants. He was, according to Jain tradition, the last in line of twenty-four *Tirthankaras* (which, literally translated, means "ford finders," or, figuratively, "saints" or "saviors"). Twenty-three Jains— "conquerors"—had preceded him, the legends related; the preceding one, Parshva, of a century or more earlier, was apparently a genuine historical person. Mahavira was known not only by that name, signifying "the great hero" and by Jina, "The Conquerer," but also as "Nataputta Vardhamana," his original name which is seldom used today.

Basic to Jain doctrine was Mahavira's belief that everything in the entire universe is eternal; to offset any views to
the contrary and to dissociate himself from the Brahmans,
he specifically included matter in this category. Spirits are
conscious of their identity, he insisted; and they retain that
consciousness through successive incarnations by the law of
karma. A man's conduct during each existence affects his
spirit for good or for ill in a later incarnation, thus having a
cumulative effect, the permanent deposit in a man's soul of
that person's deeds and actions. After knowing incarnation,
however, the Jain is able to attain nirvana and be granted
release from the body; but if the soul desires, it may, even
after the attainment of nirvana, consent to undergo additional births if such a decision helps weaker spirits in their
own search for salvation.

The Jains have always believed that the Brahman-At-
man, concerning which the Brahmans of Hinduism spoke,
did not exist at all. There is, say they, no All-One, no basic
substance holding the world and the universe in order, no
highest deity. The gods, who are higher beings and exist
on different levels within the celestial sphere, are really only
finite; they, too, have to be reborn and are therefore not
really gods, for they are neither infinite nor divine.

Only by attaining salvation on one's own could moksha,
the salvation, be achieved. Prayers were of no help, priests
of no avail. The Vedas could not be invoked, for they, said
the Jains, were neither sacred nor unique. Each man must
find salvation within himself: "Man! Thou art thine own
friend. Why wishest thou for a friend beyond thyself?"
Into this single sentence, Mahavira packed the essence of his
faith. His followers and foes alike quote it often, the former
in enthusiastic support of and the latter in derisive opposition
to Jainism.

To attain moksha, the state of liberation, the Jainist must practice asceticism, rigorously and earnestly. Twelve years of self-denial and austerity, Mahavira's own time span for successful attainment of moksha, are necessary before a man can reach nirvana. The yati (an ascetic) must take the "five great vows" prescribed for Jain monks: to injure no creature; to speak the truth; to abstain from stealing; to renounce all worldly goods; and to practice continence. In this manner only can he achieve self-mastery.

The first vow, dealing with the subject of ahimsa, or non-injury to any and all living beings, remains the most important of the five: "The first great vow, Sir, runs thus: I renounce all killing of living beings, whether movable or immovable. Nor shall I myself kill living beings nor cause others to do it, nor consent to it. As long as I live, I confess, and blame, and exempt myself of these sins, in mind, speech and body."

The renunciation of any interest in or indulgence of sexual desires—the fifth vow—is almost as important, certainly in implication if, however, not in widespread effectiveness. Mahavira was absolutely sure on one point: "The greatest temptation in the world is women . . . Men forsooth say, 'These are the vessels of happiness.' But this leads them to pain, to delusion, to death, to hell, to birth as hell-beings or brute beasts."

For average persons the Five Great Vows usually prove to be too stiff an assignment. For them, Jains have provided a less severe regimen—namely, twelve vows prescribing strict commandments not to take human or animal life, be unfaithful to a spouse, or to lie, steal, or cheat, and including positive injunctions to give alms, practice self-denial, guard against evil, meditate regularly, avoid needless travel, and restrain greed.

Most important was the first vow: not knowingly to take the life of any sentient creature, that is, any person or thing capable of feeling or perception. This prohibition meant that a man could not till the soil; nor could he engage in fishing or butchering, or follow any occupation which required the taking of life.

Many Jains had come from the warrior castes and now had to relinquish their profession of shedding blood and of killing. The merchants, however, had not been dislodged from their occupations by Jain teachings, and were able to compete with the Brahmans successfully. For the most part Jains came from the middle classes and thus had the social position to gather wealth and to achieve distinction in both literature and architecture.

There have always been two major sects among Jains, the Digambaras and the Svetambaras. These two factions differed on the matter of wearing clothes, for the Digambaras insisted that Mahavira did not wear clothes and any monk owning property or wearing clothes was therefore unable to reach nirvana. The Digambaras—the "sky-clad" or "clothed in atmosphere"—went about naked and even denied themselves food at times, but in this day they no longer practice total nudity. Women are not allowed to join the Digambara sect; denied salvation, they are forced to wait for some future reincarnation as males. The other sect, the Svetambaras, are clad in white and include both nuns and monks, who devote themselves to their sacred literature and to charitable acts.

The Jains are especially proud of the time-honored story in their writings of the six blind men who, placing their hands on different parts of the elephant, maintained that the elephant was "like a fan," "like a wall," "like a snake," "like a rope, etc." To them this parable highlights the fallacies to which all human thought falls prey, for nothing is absolutely true or false; both yes and no are proper answers to every single question. Knowledge, say the Jains, is, at best, relative and partial.

Not without reason have the Jains exerted an influence far beyond their numbers, partly by influencing philosophy, especially logic, and partly by having molded the thought of Mahatma Gandhi, for ahimsa, or the theory of non-violence, helped to formulate his spiritual views and his political policies.

Inasmuch as Jains cannot engage in any occupation which endangers life, they have had to devote themselves instead to finance and commerce. This shift in vocations and professions has resulted in their attaining unusual prosperity as lawyers and bankers, moneylenders and brokers, merchants and proprietors of land. Though they renounce the world, they are unusually rich in worldly goods; and in a land of such widespread poverty and misery as India they are a paradox of affluence.

For a number of reasons Jainism is important in our times. First of all, it is the oldest personally founded religion in India. Second, it was a conscious effort to reform or improve Hinduism; but it resulted in a new and separate religion, rather than in a reaffirmation of the best in Hinduism. Third, it has given the world an exquisite architecture. And, fourth, Jains have contributed greatly, through their influence on Gandhi and his formulation of non-violence as a political technique, to the attainment of the independence of India from British imperial rule and the assurance of India's commonwealth status in the British Commonwealth of Nations.

The second point is of greatest significance, for Jainism broke clear of Hinduism when Mahavira condemned the caste system and advocated the equality of all religious ascetics; yet only partial success resulted, for the caste system was too firmly entrenched across so many centuries and among such vast numbers of people. Despite Mahavira's denunciation of the caste system, the Jains today are a closed group.

It is important to note that Jainism does not share the beliefs of Hindus in deities, both plural and singular, but maintains instead no belief in a God or gods. In addition, ahimsa, consistent with the prohibition against destroying life, impels Jains to protest the animal sacrifices of Hinduism and to substitute kindness. Moreover, Jains do not share the Hindus' faith in the efficacy of ceremonies, rituals, and prayers, but maintain that men can attain salvation on their own; nor do the Jains agree with Hindus that Sanskrit is a sacred language, for to them it is archaic and outmoded. Mahavira taught in the language of his era and region, the vernacular called Prakit; and in that tongue his followers immortalized the writings of Jainism.

Mahavira considered the world, not his own nation or region, to be his fatherland and his homeland; he scorned the idea that a man's family or caste should be the center of his interest and loyalty. He considered his faith to be a universal religion, meant for all men and nations.

Many a visitor to a Jain temple wonders if Jains have not forgotten Mahavira's insistence on self-reliance, for the two million Jains in India have so venerated Mahavira, founder of their faith, that the veneration goes beyond even canonization and seems to approach deification. His words resound across twenty-five centuries, both as reminder and reproach, "Man! Thou art thine own friend. Why wishest thou for a friend beyond thyself?"

III
BUDDHISM

The Noble Eightfold Path

IN THE SAME century, the sixth B.C., and less than a generation after Jainism, Buddhism arose. It had many elements in common with Jainism; its central figure, Siddhartha Gautama, like Mahavira sought to liberate the true self by denying the world. He questioned the power of the Vedas, repudiated the rituals associated with them and, as a member of the Kshatriya caste, opposed the claims of the priests in the Brahman caste that only they knew the path to salvation. Gautama broadened the appeal of this new faith to include all of Indian society.

Unlike Jainism, Buddhism advocated moderation, "The Middle Path." Gautama, the Buddha, did not believe in trying to be an ascetic and he sought to avoid both extremes: asceticism and sensualism. Living in an age of social change

54

and intellectual ferment, he calmly counseled: "Follow the Middle Path. There is a Middle Path avoiding these two extremes . . . a path which opens the eyes, and bestows understanding, which leads to peace of mind, to the higher wisdom, to full enlightenment, to Nirvana . . . It is this Noble Eightfold Path; that is to say: right beliefs; right aspirations; right speech; right conduct; right livelihood; right effort; right mindfulness; and right contemplation."

Like Mahavira, Siddhartha Gautama came from a noble family, married, and had one child; but, dissatisfied with his life of privilege, he left his home, as had Mahavira, to become a wandering monk. Gautama turned his back on the accepted Hinduism of his time and began a new religion which knew no distinctions of caste and diverged sharply from Brahman practices. There the resemblance ends, for Mahavira's and Gautama's attitudes and careers diverged, just as do their respective faiths, Jainism and Buddhism, 2500 years later.

Born in 560 B.C., in a region of northern India about 100 miles from Benares, Siddhartha Gautama, as the son of King Suddhodana and Queen Maha-Maya of the Sakya clan, knew only luxury and protective care during his childhood and youth. Despite a happy marriage and the assurance of a secure, comfortable future, both as a landowner and as a ruler, he was not at ease. A lack of inner contentment disturbed him. He felt this void at the time of his marriage in his late teens but experienced it more acutely in his late twenties when he became a father. The discontent led him to the decision to leave his family—his kindly and generous father, his lovely and gracious wife, his cherished and adored child—so that he could learn of life outside the guarded walls of the palatial estates.

A familiar legend of Buddhism, "The Four Passing

Sights," describes the father's efforts to shield his son from the sordid side of life. The father of Gautama had, at the time of his son's birth, been warned that the prince might someday forsake the family, become a mendicant monk begging for alms along the road, and thus lose the opportunity destiny had in store for him of becoming "a universal monarch" as India's emperor. Carefully and intently the father kept his son from knowing the sadness and the seamy aspects of normal existence. He guarded him against seeing the inroads of disease, the erosion of age, and the tragedy of death. Amid the opulence and magnificence of three palaces, the boy grew to adulthood and knew nothing of the harshness of life, never seeing the ill or the aged and remaining unaware of the pain and disorder of the natural world.

The gods decided to send one of their own, disguised as an infirm old man, to bring the prince to reality. When the prince asked his charioteer to explain what he was now seeing for the first time, he heard an explanation of age and the inevitable, inescapable end of a man's life. A second sight, a man hideously ravaged by disease, caused him to learn how debilitated and sickened a man could be his whole life long. In a third instance he saw a corpse being carried to the cremation ground. The prince now had found out about death; in later years, he related how he had reflected: "I also am subject to decay and am not free from the power of old age, sickness and death. Is it right that I should feel horror, repulsion, and disgust when I see another in such plight? And when I reflected thus, my disciples, all the joy of life which there is in life died within me."

The king, his father, tried to bring cheer and joy to the young prince, providing entertainment and diversions but to no avail. Torn by his conflicts and racked by his lack of inner

certitude, Gautama remained distraught until the fourth
sight. As he sat beneath a tree, an ascetic dressed in a saf-
fron-colored robe came to him by the side of the road. From
him Gautama heard that a man might be freed from disease
and old age and death. In that hour and at that moment,
Gautama resolved to leave home and to wander as a monk.

This decision his father stoutly resisted and determined
to distract his son from such morbid moods. He sent dancing
girls to entertain Gautama, but they left the son unmoved
and still silently brooding. As the dancing girls became ex-
hausted and one by one fell fast asleep, Gautama waited;
when they were all sleeping, he left the room, inwardly
repelled by the silent sleepers on the floor. For the last time
he went to the apartment of his wife, looked upon the
mother and the son, Rahula, bade them a mute good-bye, and
left the house. He mounted a large white horse and galloped
far beyond the river, while the charioteer rode by his side.
Then he cut off his beard and hair—"in all the beauty of
my early prime, with a wealth of coal-black hair untouched
by gray"—and gave up his fine clothes to wear the rough
yellow robes of a wandering mendicant monk. He ordered
the charioteer to return home while he entered the forest to
begin his six years of struggle to attain salvation.

First he went to the royal city of a province called
Magadha—Rajagaya—and, following some of the yoga
methods, lived with Brahman ascetics. Their disciplines left
him unsatisfied. Stages of meditation, leading to a realm of
nothingness, or of neither perception nor nonperception, did
not satisfy his mind and spirit.

Now that he had given Brahmanism another chance and
found it would not lead him to enlightenment, he tried
Jainism. For five years, in a grove at Uruvela on the banks
of a river, he practiced such arduous self-discipline and as-

ceticism that soon he was little more than a living wraith. He found that his mind was the clearer as he disciplined his body; but he believed that if he forced his mind to dominate his heart, remaining free of all the pleasures of sense, he would find salvation. For days and months he practiced such self-domination, living on vile foods, including his own excrement, sitting on a couch of thorns, lying amid the crumbling bones and decaying flesh of corpses in a cemetery, subsisting on single grains of rice or grain. Yet the punished body, painfully thin, mercilessly disciplined, cruelly mortified, brought him no enlightenment. He then asked himself whether he should not seek other paths.

Five more ascetics gathered around him and joined in the quest. When Gautama fainted, the five thought him ready to die. Soon he revived, however, and announced that the way of mortification could not bring peace of mind. Now he would eat and drink, continuing as a begging pilgrim monk but strengthening the body so that it might support his intellect. The five ascetics, disillusioned and outraged, banned him for indulging himself in luxury. Their friend, their ideal, had succumbed to the evil of self-indulgence.

Gautama began once more, convinced that mere meditation and mortification of the body helped not at all. He started his search anew. At Buddhagaya he entered a sacred grove and sat beneath a tree which in time was described as the bo tree or the bodhi tree ("the tree of knowledge"). He vowed that he would meditate until "I attain enlightenment, . . . though skin, nerves, and bone shall waste away, and life-blood itself be dried up." He thought about his seeming failure and asked himself: what have my life and my search for the past six years accomplished?

Abruptly he discovered the answer. It had been *tanha,* his craving and his thirst, a too intent desire which had impeded him—and, for that matter, the entire human race. He, and they, had sought the wrong things. He had desired in a carnal way and thus had defeated himself. If he rid himself of that desire, he would know nirvana, complete and utterly blissful peace. This realization, ridding him of any sensual desires, purged him of what he termed "wrong states of mind." He knew an ecstasy now which was beyond either satisfaction or dissatisfaction, an elevation that gave him the purest of motives and the deepest mood of peace. Ignorance was gone and knowledge stood in its place. Darkness had vanished and light blazed forth. He felt that he had completed his rebirth and had attained the highest life. His task was finished and he had become "The Enlightened One," the Buddha.

He had, however, to share these insights, for he could not remain a Buddha for himself alone. He must teach and share and guide. He found again the five ascetics who had left him in Uruvela. Locating them in the Deer Park near Benares, he met only scorn from them at first, but he reflected such deep conviction and convincing power that he soon began to win them over.

In his famous "Sermon in the Deer Park at Sarnath near Benares," Gautama countered their accusations that his self-indulgence and non-asceticism had robbed him of enlightenment; and the five now acknowledged him to be an *arahat*— that is, a monk who had attained nirvana, or enlightenment. As they consented to try his Middle Path, founding the monastic order called the Sangha, Gautama set out on his ministry through northern India.

He found many converts in his own caste of Kshatriyas, and among lower castes as well—even among the Brahmans he instructed. He trained his monks and gathered new disciples year after year. These ten precepts guided the mem-

bers of the Sangha: refrain from destroying life [*ahimsa*];
do not take what is not given; abstain from unchastity; do
not lie or deceive; abstain from intoxicants; eat moderately
and not after noon; do not look at dancing, singing, or
dramatic spectacles; do not affect the use of garlands, scents,
unguents, or ornaments; do not use high or broad beds; do
not accept gold or silver.

The Middle Way or Path went by these ten precepts,
steering an even course between the self-indulgence which
was earnestly and specifically forbidden and the extreme
asceticism which had never been commanded.

The first five of these precepts could be obeyed by lay
associates of the Sangha order. Buddha allowed women to
form an order of nuns; but his consent was reluctant and not
without reservations, for he wryly remarked to his cousin,
Ananda, that "if women had not received permission to
enter the order, the pure religion would have lasted long, the
good law would have stood fast a thousand years. But since
they have received permission, it will now stand fast for only
five hundred years."

Almost a half century of teaching and preaching, planning and working marked the Buddha's active ministry,
and at the age of eighty he approached his life's end in a
little town named Kusinara northeast of the city of Benares.
At the home of the goldsmith Chunda, he ate his noonday
meal; but the food he ate—in some accounts pork, and in
others a dish of truffles—made him ill. As he lay on the
ground between two sal trees, not far from Kusinara, he
died.

Two major rejections and two major acceptances were the
four cornerstones on which he built his structure of thought,
expecting his disciples to elaborate it.

The two rejections were: his denial that philosophical

speculation was of any value in finding salvation, and his
turning away from bhakti—religious piety and devotion—
as a means of attaining salvation. Concerned with practical
and human issues, he had little patience with a projection
of the mind into the realm of metaphysics (that branch of
philosophy which deals with first principles and seeks to explain the nature of being or reality, the origin of the world,
and what constitutes knowledge). Nor did he believe in
prayer or the holiness of the Vedas, the worth of rituals or
the aristocratic prestige of a priestly caste like the Brahmans.
He was a non-theistic humanist and, like Mahavira, he
urged his followers to look to their own strength and resources for salvation. Such views were heretical to the Hindus, especially to devoutly observant followers of Hinduism.

Yet two basic tenets of Hinduism he accepted, modifying
each: the law of karma and the transmigration of beings. In
the case of the former, the law of karma, he believed that if
a man altered his ways, experienced a change of heart which
brought new directions and new objectives, "the state of
him that is worthy," he would not have visited upon him
the penalty for sins he had committed in an earlier existence.
This assertion created controversy among his followers for
hundreds of years thereafter—and does so to this day. Those
who have become steadfast of mind and therefore are rid of
evil desire need concern themselves no longer about karma,
he taught, for none is needed any longer; they need no
rebirth and are exempt from any longing for a future life.
These, the wise, "are extinguished at death like a lamp"
and will not know a rebirth. Only those who are still burdened with *tanha,* the thirst to live and the craving to have,
will be reborn.

Behind all this reflection on the need of, or the exemption
from, rebirth lay the Buddha's basic conviction that the

world around and within us is in flux, an endless process of change and decay, of coming and going, of becoming and vanishing. There is no basic Reality, no inherent Intelligence, no Supreme Personality at the heart and essence of existence. Being is basically and ultimately impersonal. Nirvana, illimitably pure and all-embracing, is the goal, for it brings peace to the self which no longer thinks of itself as an ego. This *dhamma,* the doctrine of the turning of the wheel, points to the never-ending becoming, rather than fulfillment, the never-ceasing change, which reveals how impermanent is the seemingly permanent. Dhamma brings the pain of knowing only incompletion, partial realization, and inevitable failures to attain the whole or the perfect. Buddha felt that men erred in clinging to the pleasures of life. So painful is existence and so wearisome is this yearning to hold to the world we know and experience consciously that it is best for men to allow it to perish; then they need not be compelled to seek rebirth.

When Buddha preached his first sermon to the five ascetics in the Deer Park, he gave an answer to the perplexing problem: "How should one live so that he might diminish pain and suffering, might destroy the deplorable 'will-to-live-and-have' [*tanha*], and thus know liberation and its joy?"

He answered by describing the Four Noble Truths: suffering, cause of suffering, cessation of suffering, and the noble truth of the path which led to an ever lessening suffering, namely the Noble Eightfold Path—right beliefs, right aspiration, right speech, right conduct, right means of livelihood, right effort, right mindfulness, right contemplation.

To the average man in the Western world, the ethics of Buddha seem to be negative and pessimistic; but this is an inaccurate judgment. Buddha may appear to have been negative in his counsels; but he had a positive objective: spiritual happiness or "blessedness." Not all existence leads to misery, not all desire is wrong. The wise man, having overcome ignorance, is able to determine what is not miserable in existence and what is admirable in desire. To avoid suffering and cause no suffering, he advised: "Let therefore no man love anything: loss of the beloved is evil. Those who love nothing and hate nothing have no fetters."

When Buddha urged that a person break the bonds which tie him to the wheel of existence, he sought to lift "ten fetters": (1) belief in the existence of the self, (2) doubt, (3) trust in ceremonies of good works, (4) lust, (5) anger, (6) desire for rebirth in worlds of form, (7) desire for rebirth in formless worlds, (8) pride, (9) self-righteousness, and (10) ignorance.

The goal of the Noble Eightfold Path, "the path that leads to no-desire," is sainthood or the state of an *arahat;* the "worthy" man who has attained nirvana, a level of calm and joy, of energy and benevolence (*sambodhi*) and who is freed from desires that bring misery. Calmly and fearlessly continuing to "put out the lamp of life," he awaits *parinirvana,* the ultimate nirvana upon his death. There is no more transmigration then, no pain and misery in becoming or in mere being. Perfect happiness is at hand.

At the heart of Buddhism are good will, benevolence, compassion for all men. "Love all mankind with a mother's love" is a central commandment. Many a sentence from Buddha's lips sounds similar to the words of Jesus in his Sermon on the Mount. As Buddha reminded his followers, "Hatred ceases by love, this is an old rule." He admonished, "If someone curses you, you must repress all resentment"; so Jesus spoke six centuries later and three thousand miles distant.

Yet how can one break fetters and allow no attachments as Buddha bade men do, when his all-embracing love is sought? This inconsistency created a fissure in Buddhism, the historic division between the *Hinayana* and the *Mahayana*.

Broadly speaking, Hinayana Buddhism is the more conservative of the two. It centers on the role of the monk and his search for "arahatship" or sainthood. It focuses on meditation, mendicancy, and the striving for liberation with a life bent on gathering merit for ultimate salvation. The doctrine of the Hinayana Buddhists is much more "religious" than Buddha's precepts; Hinayanists revere Buddha through both reputed relics of him and an extraordinary number of images of Buddha, ranging in every size from the infinitesimal to the gigantic. The Hinayana monk considers Buddha to have entered nirvana and therefore to be at peace, exempt from the problems of being-and-becoming and beyond the knowledge of being. The universe and all who exist within it—men and animals, gods and spirits—are in process of changing and this means suffering.

Hinayana Buddhism prevails today in Thailand, Burma, Cambodia, Ceylon, and Laos. Literally translated as "the Lesser Vehicle," it interprets salvation as attainable by personal effort and urges the individual to austerity. The welfare of others is not the goal. Hinayana Buddhists do not care, however, for the designation of their older and more cautious Buddhism as the Lesser Vehicle (for *yana* signifies a means of transportation and *Hinayana* implies the use of a Lesser Raft or Lesser Ferry to cross the river into nirvana). They prefer to call themselves the Theravada Buddhists— *Theravada* meaning "the teaching of the elders."

The Mahayana Buddhists, however, have always liked the term "the Greater Vehicle," for the phrase implied that

salvation was open to all and could be universally achieved.
A Mahayanist sought to become a Buddha, the possibility
open to everyone. He might not achieve it during a single
lifetime; but the steps, numbering ten, were carefully outlined and everyone was eligible to apply. Here was salvation
by both faith and good works. Not only monks could apply
but all laymen as well. Take the vow to become a Buddha
and assume the name "Bodhisattva." In due time, the vow
taker could become a "cosmic helper"—that is, one devoted
to saving mankind. Mahayana Buddhism, more altruistic,
began to flourish in northwest India and became so attractive
in its openness that it then spread to China, Korea, Japan,
Mongolia, and Tibet.

The Mahayanists created their own scriptures. They
took a part from the Theravada (or Hinayana) canon; but
they developed their own Mahayana books which empha-
size the tradition that Gautama had been preceded by many
other Buddhas, some on the earth and some still in the
heavens, but with more Buddhas still to come in the future.
Five major Buddhas, including Gautama, had already
arrived. One Buddha, named Maitreya, was still to appear.

The Hinayana Buddhists had adhered to "the teaching
of the elders" when, in the fifth century B.C., some monks
tried to ease the severe restrictions of Buddhist discipline; in
response they, the Hinayanists, resisted. Many divisive
movements arose within Buddhism in the following decades
and might have destroyed the movement from within if
Asoka had not ascended the throne in 273 B.C. to become
one of the greatest emperors in the history of India.

Asoka, like his famous grandfather, Chandragupta, conquered enemies ruthlessly and completely; but when Asoka
accepted Buddhism, he was transformed into a man of
peace. Now he was opposed to warfare and violence. He

propagated this new faith, first by expressing his genuine
and profound regrets for having killed and displaced so
many hundreds of thousands of people, and then by vowing
to be gentle, meek, and patient from that time on. He
abolished the royal hunt, forbade the slaughter of animals,
and urged all his people to be good Buddhists. Everywhere
in his kingdom he built temples and schools, cultivated trees
and provided water, constantly building monuments on
which he inscribed the precepts of Buddhism. Then he sent
missionaries into other lands, not only to Ceylon and Burma
but also to the Greek kingdoms in Asia and Europe and
to Egypt in North Africa. His missionaries to Western
lands seem not to have been successful, but the dominance
of Hinayana Buddhism in Burma and Ceylon, Thailand
and Cambodia, is apparent even now, a testimony to his
new-found faith and the power it exerted in his life.

Mahayana Buddhism—"the Greater Vehicle"—
stretched out toward the north of India and then, apparently
in the first century B.C., spread into China. Then it moved
into Korea; and from both Korea and China, especially the
latter, it came to Japan. Its entry into Tibet caused it to
merge with the religions of that area, perhaps with some
version of early Christianity, a merger that resulted in a
Buddhism entirely different from that in other lands.
Tibetan Buddhism bears the name of Lamaism where the
chief figure, the Dalai Lama, is venerated as a Bodhisattva.

Meanwhile Buddhism encountered troubles in India. It
may have expanded successfully and even triumphantly
throughout other parts of the Orient; but in India it had
difficulties, so that in the century after Asoka's death powerful influences against it began to arise. By a thousand years
after Asoka it had vanished in India, in part because Hinduism, from which it had originally sprung, absorbed Bud-

dhism and its distinctive nature; and partly because the armies of Islam invaded India in the twelfth century and destroyed whatever remained of Buddhism. The influence and spread of Buddhism outside of India, however, became greater with the passing of the centuries.

A by-product of Mahayana Buddhism is Zen Buddhism, which is quite popular in Western countries. Paradoxically, it really resembles Hinayana Buddhism because of its austerity and its belief that a flash of intuition, occurring during carefully disciplined meditation, brings enlightenment.

Zen Buddhism developed in the latter part of the sixth century A.D., when Bodhidharma came to China, shortly after the conversion of the Emperor Wu Ti to Buddhism. According to a generally accepted legend the Emperor called Bodhidharma from North China to question him about the merit which would come from his donating to Buddhist monks and encouraging the translation of sacred works. Bodhidharma, dour and blunt, answered, "No merit at all." He told the Emperor that good works and wide reading were useless; only through meditation would His Majesty know anything about the reality of Buddha. To prove his point to the skeptical king, Bodhidharma went to Mount Su and, for the next nine years, faced a wall in meditation, maintaining perfect silence.

Zen spread to Japan some centuries later. Zen Buddhists refused to define the Buddha principle and scorned all scriptures; they held an iconoclastic attitude toward life and encouraged complete individualism. In its varied kinds of meditation and its several divisions, Zen affected Japanese religion greatly, bringing its influence to bear on Shinto, a religion native to Japan. Zen's plain living, plus rigorous self-discipline in preparation for prolonged meditation and an inward vision, appealed greatly to Japanese warriors in the twelfth and subsequent centuries. It encouraged single-minded thought about sacrifice of the self and the devotion of a man to his native land and to his emperor.

Zen did more, however, for it highlighted the importance of intuition, especially in imagining and then designing houses and temples, planning household furnishings and civic buildings, arranging flowers and retaining a restrained attitude toward life. The relation of the Zen novice to a Zen master, as the master rebukes or rejects him, kicks him or slaps him, is a clue to some of the intricacies of Zen.

Many keenly intellectual, highly cultured Orientals, as well as sensitive, knowledgeable intellectuals of the Western world, find the mental and spiritual self-discipline of Zen appealing. They look to it as a way of guidance in a thing-centered, seemingly purposeless world. Books and views, discussions and preachments mean little to Zen monks or their disciples. To them involved questions and obscure, puzzling riddles are much more effective in probing for truth.

The essential principle of Zen is apparent in the story of a disciple of Buddha who brought him a golden flower as a gift and asked him to reveal the secret of his outlook. Taking the flower, Buddha held it high and looked at it silently. In this way he indicated that his secret could not be found in words but rather in contemplating the flower in all its beauty and meaning.

Buddhism came back to India by a recent turn of significant events when Dr. Bhimrao Ramji Ambedkar, the leader of the untouchables, chose to convert himself and his followers to Buddhism. This mass conversion of the untouchables to Buddhism in 1954 occurred after Dr. Ambedkar passed through a period of crisis. He could have adopted Christianity or Islam, but decided in favor of Buddhism because it was native to India and thus was very close to the Hinduism in which these untouchables had been reared. Not all the untouchables followed into this new grouping (called the Neo-Buddhist), because they wanted to remain Hindus and hoped to reform Hinduism from within. But that this dramatic choice of Buddhism occurred among such a downtrodden, exploited group was a striking example of the Buddha's power after 2,500 years.

In many parts of East Asia, Buddhism is faced by the challenge of other religions: in Japan where the "new religions" are a diversion and a counterforce; in China and Tibet, where the Communist regime has been increasingly hostile and repressive, but where tens of millions seem to have a nominal, though wistful, attachment and apparently contrive some observance of its traditional rites.

In other parts of Asia, especially in southeast Asia, Buddhism has revived. Ironically, the presence of Christian missionaries intent on making conversions of their own caused Buddhists to be aware of their faith, to rethink it, and to adhere all the more firmly to it. Asians of education and culture felt impelled to read anew, to translate afresh, and to provide commentaries for their own classics. Soon they became alert to the spiritual wealth in the Buddhist tradition.

Hinayana Buddhism has become stronger and healthily self-conscious with the firm establishment of Asian nationhood in such lands as Burma, Thailand, and Ceylon. When combined with the vast social changes brought about by industrialization and the ideals of economic justice and social equality, whether promised by Western democratic nations or repeated in the slogans of Communist countries, Buddhism has found fresh strength and new purpose.

Buddhist scholars throughout Asia now seek to bridge the chasm between Hinayana and Mahayana Buddhism and minimize the great differences that prevailed through many centuries; they tend to interpret the two sectors as complementing each other and having inherited a common lode of spiritual treasure. The great conference of Buddhists, gathered in the Sixth Buddhist Council at Rangoon from 1954 to 1956 to celebrate the twenty-five hundredth anniversary of Gautama's birth, gave stimulus to the Buddhist enterprise and encouraged Buddhists to lay plans for further missionary work throughout the world—as witnessed by more than one hundred missionaries of Buddhism working in the United States and Canada and by the return of many missionaries to India, the land of Buddhism's origin.

The growing response to Buddhism in many lands is proof that the Noble Eightfold Path has both meaning and appeal to many tens of millions in our time.

IV
CONFUCIANISM
AND
TAOISM

The Will of Heaven

CONFUCIUS and Lao Tse, contemporaries of the sixth century B.C., seem never to have met, save once, if a vague legend is right; but their parallel, though differing, lines of thought bridged the remote past of vast China's realm into their own present and on into a future of 2,500 years more, down to our present day. Their basic traditions, "Confucianism" and "Taoism" as we call them, combined at times with certain aspects of Buddhism; all three, unconsciously and without organized pattern, colored the thought and conduct of countless millions of Chinese across more than a hundred generations.

Both Confucius and Lao Tse would have agreed on one fact: thousands of years from the Chinese past had molded the outlooks of both, individual and unique though each was.

They looked back to what they knew to have been at least 1,500 years of a rich, elaborate culture, and recalled at least 4,000 years of recorded history from their time. Charming myths explained the origins and were redolent of a history which extended over ten epochs of at least two million years (and in another version, ninety-six million years).

The ancient Chinese saw order and interdependence and unity in all the processes of heaven and earth: the stars in their courses and the seasons in their cycles. Man was to harmonize his actions with the laws of heaven and earth. Otherwise, Heaven would punish the disruptions by the sending of disasters. Harmony would again prevail only if man acted in consonance with nature. Such was the Will of Heaven.

Reflection on these miracles and on these mysteries of nature and of the universe led some ancient Chinese thinkers, unknown and unnamed to us, to formulate the concept that every object knew the interacting forces of *yin* and *yang*.

Yin was the female principle in nature. Here was an element measured in its pace, low in key, wet and cold, secretive and mysterious, fecund and brooding. Yin was to be found amid quietude, among shadows. Yin was the south bank of a river in shadow. It was the north side of a hill in shelter.

Yang, in turn, was considered to be the masculine element. It called forth such adjectives as positive, procreative, warm and dry, active and bright. Yang was the south side of a hill. It was the north side of a river. Fire and sunlight were yang.

Each object had both yin and yang. The log in the wood-pile was yin in appearance but became yang when kindled into fire. People, were they men or women, possessed both, though the men more of yang and the women more of yin. Yet the Chinese thought that good spirits (*shen*) were yang in nature, and evil spirits (*kwei*) were yin.

When asked why, Chinese philosophers of long ago answered, "*Tao.*" In Tao (pronounced "Dow") reposed the unity of yin and yang, of heaven and earth. Tao, "the way," implied the road or direction they were to follow if they were to fulfill their function in the plan of the universe. When men rebelled against that pattern or were goaded by devilish spirits to recalcitrance, heaven and earth and mankind were not in harmony and the universal well-being of all three was threatened, often shattered. Like almost all religions, early Chinese beliefs harked back to a golden era; earth had been a paradise and men had lived in blissful peace and accord.

The earliest traces of Chinese worship reveal ceremonies in honor of the earth and its fertility, heaven and its beneficent rains; the rites honored the spirits to be found in the fields, rivers, roads, valleys, and mountains, but guarded also against wild animals and unfriendly spirits in swamps, caves, and stagnant water.

The Chinese folk religion began to gravitate then toward ancestor worship. In that manner could the living pay honor to their entire relationship from which had come both physical life and spiritual legacies. By the same token the departed could, in the link with posterity through sacrifices and prayers, strengthen and guide the living, enhance their happiness, bring prosperity. By visits to graves and by recounting the lives of ancestors, those who were alive might honor the dead and re-establish their sense of continuity with earlier generations.

An elaborate gradation of classes, ranging from the emperor down to the vassals and the most menial of serfs, lay imbedded in the feudal order of 3,000 and more years ago. In the eighth century B.C. this class structure, once so rigid and prescribed, began to crumble. The aristocrats became poor and upstarts of lowlier rank clambered for position and privilege. The serfs shook off their fetters to become small landowners; indeed some of them eventually became men of property.

During the five centuries of slow but steady change, of reshuffling and readjusting, the basic schools of thought of the Confucianists and of the Taoists emerged: the Confucianists seem to have been furthered by princes and dukes and to have come from the region of the Yellow River, while the Taoists appear to have included many cynical, disillusioned intellectuals and to have had most of their followers in the area of the Yangtze River. Origins of both regions and ideas may be debatable, but it is clear that the Confucianists opposed the group called Legalists, who wanted to wipe out the feudal structure. The Confucianists, following the aristocratic Confucianists, sought to restore feudalism, but they wanted a modified, reformed system. In contrast, the Taoists wanted to rid the land and their time of any order which might be highly centralized. A smaller group, the Mohists, desired a reversion to the bygone days when they, as farmers and craftsmen, depended on the universal benevolence for their happiness and prosperity.

In such an era of rebuilding and recasting, Confucianism evolved. So powerful was the influence of Confucius himself, so all-pervading were his life and character, so inextricably entwined were his ideas in Chinese social institutions—especially in the family and the government—that for scores of generations after his death he still shaped the education, the conduct, and the politics of China. These environmental supports fitted in with the objective needs of Chinese society for almost 2,500 years.

In the modern period as China's social structure began to undergo radical change, Confucian institutions no longer served life's needs in Chinese society; consequently Confucianism declined. Even with the complete revival and resurrection of Confucianism in our time—an unlikely possibility under any consideration—its former pre-eminent position could never be restored.

In our time, men and women in certain parts of the Orient—especially in Taiwan (Formosa)—look to the tradition of Confucius for guidance and inspiration; they avow their intention to do so, if not impeded or interrupted by an invading conque.or, for untold years to come. The intense opposition of Mao Tse-tung's Red Guards to Confucianism, even to its last vestiges of belief and its final remnants of adherence, reveals in fact the tenacity of Confucianists and affirms the durable qualities of the faith "Master K'ung" began in the sixth century B.C.

Confucius, or K'ung Fu-tse as he was called in Chinese, was born in 551 B.C. in a town called T-sou, in a county named Ch'angping in the province of Lu in the Shantung Peninsula. His ancestors had fled there to a new but poverty-ridden existence as a result of a revolution in the area. After his father's death, Confucius supported his mother; she in turn saw to it that her son had the requisite teaching and tutoring he needed to know ancient China's music, history, and poetry. Trained also to be a sportsman, fisherman, hunter, and archer, Confucius adhered to the standards of both scholar and gentleman. He endured an unsuccessful marriage, which did, however, grant him the boon of a son to preserve the ancestral ties. The sorrowful occasion of his mother's death plunged him into the traditional twenty-seven months—and even longer—of mourning, and then he became a teacher of the Six Disciplines: poetry, music, history, government, etiquette, and divination (foretelling the future).

Confucius now openly and frankly aspired for higher office in the government so that his views might affect an era so obviously in transition. He rose through the ministries of public works and justice to become the chief justice in his state; but he soon became a victim of intrigues and lost his position and prestige. With several disciples as companions, he began a long period of wandering in search of a new position. Sometimes he met with a friendly, hospitable reception; at other times he encountered contempt and violence, sarcasm and taunts.

Toward the close of his life, in 484 B.C., he received an appointment in the government of Duke Ai to a prestigious post which enabled him to spend the remaining years of his life, 484 B.C. to 479 B.C., in compiling the material we know as the Confucian Classics: *The Book of History (Shu-Ching), The Book of Poetry (Shih-Ching), The Book of Rites (Li-Chi), The Book of Changes (I-Ching),* and *The Annals of Spring and Autumn (Ch'un Ch'iu).* The last book was his own writing, while the other four were anthologies of wisdom from pre-Confucian times. A sixth work, the *Book of Music (Yueh-Ching),* though fragmentary, is reputed to have been compiled by him.

Some scholars maintain that Confucius only used these materials and did not even assemble them. He may have edited, changed, and even added to them; but they were, we are told, not his own. It is true that proofs of his authorship and editorial hand are few and, at best, flimsy. Yet this fact remains: he drew the necessary inferences from them and, with some degree of originality, uttered statements which were recorded by his disciples in *The Analects of Confucius (Lun Yü)*. "I believe in and have a passion for the ancients," he often said with due deference to the past; and with the honesty of an authentic editor he was accustomed to say, as in the *Analects,* "I am a transmitter and not a creator."

Confucianists of later centuries carried on the traditions through the *Four Books,* of which the *Analects* is closest to Confucius' mind and times, closer than the other three; one of the other three was known as *The Great Learning (Ta-Hsueh)* and is attributed to Confucius, but was probably prepared by one of his disciples. It appears to have been Tzu Ssu, the grandson of Confucius, who assembled statements about human nature in relation to the universe and its basic moral order in *The Doctrine of the Mean (Chung Yung)*; but even this supposition is not verified. A valuable book of the third century B.C., *The Book of Mencius,* was a record of the teachings of Mencius, whose philosophic relation to Confucius was like that of Plato to Socrates. Many additions, offered by later Confucianists and altered by conflicting opinions, brought varying views for almost two thousand years; but certain central ideas of Confucius stood out clearly and forcefully.

The basic concept of Confucianism was *jen,* which is variously translated as benevolence, true manhood, human-heartedness, altruistic steadfastness, uprightness of character; but is probably best rendered as humanity, namely the quality that makes man human, renders him different from animals. When applied to specific human relations *jen,* a general and all-inclusive concept, becomes *te* or "virtues." *Jen* has to do with inner feelings, not the norms of external behavior.

Confucius urged a second and very significant concept upon his corrupt era—and thus upon all succeeding generations as well—namely the necessity of living by *li*. This is translated in a number of ways: "reverence" or "propriety," "the ideal forms of social ceremonies for the proper forms of public conduct," "the courtesy of all social and religious behavior," or "the moral and religious way of life." Through *li,* society would be reordered and kept intact. Thereby, explained Confucius, men would give due and proper reverence to the spirit of the universe, honor the emperor and his advisers, establish proper moral standards for both sexes, as well as for children and parents, and ensure that all men would live in harmony and establish the proper social institutions. If *li* prevails, he maintained, all of life from birth to death, from sports to business, from attendance at the emperor's court to diplomatic protocol, will be favorably fashioned and affirmed. *Li* establishes total harmony—in the home, in the village, in the empire—and ensures *Tao,* the Will of Heaven, and its cosmic harmony between heaven and earth.

Confucius believed in the social order of his time wherein the superior and the inferior remained in their accorded places and followed the formal accepted patterns of politeness and procedures prevalent among all men at that time. As in all other religions, the Golden Rule was inherent in these admonitions; and, as is characteristic in a number of other religions, Confucius defined it negatively. When referring to "reciprocity" (*shu*), he cautioned: "What you do not want done to yourself, do not do to others."

In *The Doctrine of the Mean,* however, Confucius stated the matter in positive fashion; at least his followers accredit him in *The Conduct of Life* with this more direct way of praising *shu:* "There are four things in the moral life of

man, not one of which I have been able to carry out in my
life. To serve my father as I would expect my son to serve
me: that I have not been able to do. To serve my sovereign
as I would expect a minister under me to serve me: that I
have not been able to do. To act towards my elder brother as
I would expect my younger brother to act towards me: that
I have not been able to do. To be the first to behave towards
friends as I would expect them to behave towards me: that I
have not been able to do."

To Confucius *shu,* reciprocity, impelled men to seek *li,*
the noblest propriety or reverence, by the Ten Proper Attitudes which result in the Five Relationships: (1) kindness
in the father, and filial piety in the son; (2) gentility in the
eldest brother, and humility and respect in the younger;
(3) righteous behavior in the husband, and obedience in
the wife; (4) humane consideration in elders, and deference
in juniors; (5) benevolence in rulers, and loyalty in minis-
ters and subjects. Then would harmony prevail among all
men and the real character (*jen*) of a man would be revealed. The practice of *jen* and *li* might vary according to
social status and human relationships, but one could always
rely on *shu,* the unifying principle of reciprocity.

Confucius' ideal was the *chun-tzu*—the superior man—
who, by following these injunctions, could achieve the "Five
Constant Virtues": self respect, magnanimity, sincerity,
earnestness, and benevolence.

These were the goals for Confucius, too, who performed
his duties with *jen* (the principles of genuine manhood and
uprightness), without arrogance or boasting, but with the
assurance of one who knew *li* (the proper attitude), and
tried to fulfill *shu* (reciprocity).

As one who had attained the blessed man's "three score
years and ten," Confucius was able to say, we are told in the

Analects: "At fifteen, I had my mind bent on learning. At thirty, I stood firm. At forty, I had no doubts. At fifty, I knew the decree of Heaven. At sixty, my ear was an obedient organ for the reception of truth. At seventy, I could do what my heart desired without transgressing what was right."

It might appear that Confucius taught essentially ethics and little else. Yet such an assertion would be both inaccurate and inadequate, for at heart he was a man of faith; he was a believer in religious ceremonies and in the reality of religion. Those who rely solely on reason and those who deny the existence of a God claim him as their own. They are not wrong, for Confucius was indeed both a rationalist and a humanist. He used the mind to analyze and appraise religion, to temper enthusiasms and to restrain acceptance of the improbable or incredible. To Confucius, life's central purpose was to serve humankind. Over and over again he would say: "To devote oneself earnestly to one's duty to humanity, and, while respecting the spirits [of the dead], to keep aloof from them, may be called wisdom."

Confucius did not believe in the supernatural—that is, as we define it in the West, namely the intervention of supernatural forces in nature or phenomena which exist or occur outside the normal experience and knowledge of men. Nor did he have anything more than a faint belief in the mystical, that is, the mysteries beyond human comprehension or the experiences by which a man intuitively grasps truths beyond human understanding. His focus centered on issues and individuals having relation to human welfare. As for Heaven and its Will, he believed and taught that the Will of Heaven was fulfilled when a man practiced the moral law. His conviction that his precepts were backed by the very nature of the universe and were in accord with the

Will of Heaven made him one of the foremost religionists of Asia in all its recorded history.

After the death of Confucius, divisions in the ranks of his followers caused differing schools of thought to form. His disciples gathered in bands of the faithful and split that faith into various groups; they gathered the sayings and teachings of Confucius into the books listed earlier in this chapter and prepared still more documents (which were lost and have thus not come down to us through the centuries).

Among the rival faiths were the powerful Taoists, with ideas contemporary with Confucianism and equally famous, honorable antecedents. Taoists, who had only disdain for the Confucians, were part of a larger movement known as Taoism (pronounced "Dow-ism") the system of thinking and living where the Tao was at the core. The founding spirit of Taoism was the legendary Lao Tse, who was born, according to some traditions, at least a half century before Confucius, that is, 604 B.C. If we are to believe other scholars, the correct date is 570 B.C. Yet more recent research convinces many that the Lao Tse we refer to as the progenitor of Taoism lived in the fourth century B.C., that is about 200 years after Confucius. Any one of the three hypotheses is acceptable, for the correct date has little relation to the spread of Taoism in later centuries. Lao Tse himself is important, however, because of the ideas he represented.

For many years in the sixth century B.C., Lao Tse is said to have occupied the position as curator at the imperial archives in Loyang, capital city of the state of Ch'u. Doubtful of the need for any kind of government, he resigned from his post. Convinced that the quest for knowledge was futile and only perverted the simple life which men were destined to follow, he decided to go away. Irritated by questions from the curious, angered by the invasion of his privacy by visitors (including, according to one tradition, Confucius himself), "The Old Man" fled.

The most picturesque of the tales about Lao Tse describes the black oxen drawing the two-wheeled carriage as he prepared to depart by the western gate, happily leaving behind him the world of noise and anxiety, disease and folly. But Yin-hsi, his friend who guarded the gate at the western exit, persuaded him that he should write for posterity the philosophy he taught and lived. Lao Tse consented and stayed on in the gate house just long enough to write his *Treatise of the Tao and Its Power (Tao Te Ching)*. The sentences and paragraphs were brief and taut, though many of them were far from clear; but he had fulfilled his promise. Then he went through the gate, out into the western pass, and over the horizon, never to be heard from again.

While these details are not historically verifiable, this much is certain: *Tao Te Ching,* the classic explanation and expression of Taoism, came from a later century, as the internal evidence of language and the references to current events attest. When it was written is unimportant. What it had to say is all important. Taoism now had a Testament, and the leading thinkers of "philosophical" Taoism now had a weapon by which they could struggle against the Confucianists who had their own canons.

Difficult though the Tao might be to define, Taoists nonetheless did define it as the mystery of the cosmos which, when plumbed, resulted in even more mystery. This was the ultimate reality, the substance, the vital principle. For the Taoist it was important to be in accord with the Tao, the only way to know well-being: harmony and health and abundance. If a man or a nation, a culture or a civilization, rebelled against the course of events and moved in opposition to everlasting Tao, pain and disaster would result.

In the *Tao Te Ching* the Taoist read that if he refrained from interfering in people's lives, succumbing to anger, falling prey to ambition, the results would be not negative but positive. The result of the positive force would be favorable and beneficent. If a man allowed himself to be imbued with Tao, he would have a long life, free from illness and decay.

In the larger sphere of governing society, the same principle as applied to governing one's self was valid. The major way to freedom and peace was not to interfere in the lives of the people: "If kings and princes could but hold fast to this principle, all things would work out their own reformation."

The leading light among the Taoists was Chuang-Tzu, who lived in the fourth century, about a century after Lao Tse. With rare wit, apt illustrations, and delightful dialogues, he wrote essays to combat the Confucianism of his time. He progressed beyond the Taoism of the past, however, and wrote of change taking place naturally, all in accord with Tao. He differed from the Confucians by insisting that men could be natural and simple and just, merely by reverting to their basic natures and simple living. He loved nature and thought of it as the chief fount of imagination and of inspiration, a reflection of Tao, so awesome and mysterious, yet so lovely and ordered. He inspired the poets and artists of his people to gaze upon nature and interpret it as an outer manifestation, but nonetheless a true mirror of Tao.

Later, Taoism thrived on using magic and alchemy to seek the elixir of life in search of immortality. In the second century A.D. Emperor Huan of the second Han Dynasty decreed that Lao Tse be honored by a temple and by official gifts. Five centuries more went by, however, before an emperor made Taoism the official imperial religion.

Meanwhile, *Mahayana* Buddhism had been introduced into China from India and had spread swiftly through China and on into Korea and Japan. It was a period of strife and hardship. The people found Confucianism to be too mundane to satisfy religious yearnings, while, to the masses, philosophical Taoism had seemed too intellectual and too obscure. Mahayana Buddhism met their needs more adequately, they felt, because of the spiritual help they were assured they received daily from the Bodhisattvas and the promise of Paradise from the Dhyani Buddhas.

Challenged by Buddhism, Taoism now looked to the past and found strength in becoming an institutionalized religion. The Taoists lifted Lao Tse to a new level of respect, even of reverence. They gathered their writings into books, built temples, formed orders of disciples, and brought their several spirits and gods into an ordered pantheon. To all of this the people responded, and Taoism had a strong counter to the established Confucianism of the past and the Buddhism of much more recent vintage.

None of the three religions—Confucianism, Taoism, and Mahayana Buddhism—required exclusive allegiance; and thus every Chinese could be something of all three, depending upon the area of life affected, his temperament and mood, his success or failure, and his preference. Religion with the Chinese is a matter of viewpoint and emphasis. It can shift from day to day, from moment to moment or from activity to activity or inactivity. Such permissiveness in polyreligious views and adherences is something unknown to our own experience with Judaism or Christianity in the West.

Among the rival groups of those centuries the Mohists were important, but neither in numbers nor in influence could they claim victory over the Confucianists. Fired by the thoughts and enthusiasms of Mo-tzu of the fifth century B.C., the Mohists struggled against Confucianism. Unknown to most people now and only dimly explained in history, Mo-tzu led his followers in a highly disciplined way and looked to the day when men would be united for the common good in a brotherhood of companions. He believed that universal love came from heaven and pleaded for the simple, thrifty life, stripped of all formality and rituals. Opposed by both Taoists and Confucians, the Mohists were foiled in their teaching and living a doctrine of the universal love.

The Legalists, more powerful than the Mohists, were no less articulate in speaking and writing about their concepts. Their school of law believed the crumbling feudalism of that day should be succeeded by a strong all-inclusive law as the basis of a new social order. Confucianism was too elementary. The Taoists had interpreted the Tao too simply. Their own interpretation of the Tao, they maintained, demanded that the prince should control all government. The Legalists actually triumphed briefly over Confucianism in the third century B.C.

A century after Confucius had died, Mencius, well-known writer of Confucian thinking, came on the scene to share the belief of Confucius in man's goodness and the ability of feudalism to elicit that goodness. Coupled with his faith in man's essential goodness was the conviction that environment was responsible for man's evil and that proper environments would work for good. He followed Confucius in claiming that Heaven created the disposition for the good and the creative; he opposed the Taoists by contending that within each man lay a strong inclination to create moral order. He influenced the Chinese for hundreds of years by his insistence on the presence of a vital energy, great and powerful, in each person and in the universe. The Taoists might find this energy in nature outside themselves, but

Mencius said it flowed deep within himself and all men. His teachings are so significant in Confucian thought that he occupies a place second only to Confucius.

A contemporary of Mencius, but ranked on the opposite side, was Hsün-tzu, who was exposed to many influences, especially from the Taoists and the Legalists. Unlike Mencius he had no illusions about human nature. He focused entirely on its weakness and inherent evil. Believing that man was bad by nature, Hsün-tzu went further than Confucius in emphasizing *li,* the proprieties, and in relying on ceremonies and law to control the behavior of the people. He followed the Taoists in looking upon Heaven as being impersonal and considered *li* to be simply ornaments in civilized life to give proper expression to man's emotions.

When the Chinese Revolution of the twentieth century confronted these religions of China's past, there was an inevitable and inescapable clash. Little understanding evolved. No real meeting of Chinese minds resulted. No bridging of the canyon caused by a centuries-old difference was even possible at that time—nor does it seem to be possible in the foreseeable future. When the Chinese Communists finally assumed full control of mainland China in 1949, the last stand of the Confucianists meant ultimate defeat. (Taoism was, at best, only a cultural hangover.) Yet the strains of Confucianism are visible in the culture of China as a nation—as well as of its people. These are more than vestiges. They are an ineradicable part of China's past and, it would appear, of her future too.

V

SHINTO

The Way of the Gods

THE WORD "Shinto" reflects the religious faith of the Japanese people in their country, its origin and its past, and it bespeaks Japan's special blessedness at the hands of the divinities. In the Japanese language Shinto means "the way of the gods" (*Kami-no-michi,* i.e., the way of those "above") but when translated into Chinese, the words emerge as *"shen-tao"* and refer to Taoism.

The sacred scriptures and historic sources of Shinto are four in number: two sagas from the eighth century A.D. (*Koji-ki, The Records of Ancient Events,* and *Nihon-gi, The Chronicles of Japan*—from A.D. 712 and 720 respectively and considered to be the two chief bodies of scripture), another from the ninth century (*Manyo-shiu, The Collection of Ten Thousand Leaves*), and the fourth from the tenth century (*Yengi-shiki, The Institutes of the Period of Yengi*—from A.D. 901 to 923); they tell the story of how these lovely islands became a unique creation of the gods. Here are legends of the land's founding and the national religion's beginnings, prayers for ceremonies and important events, as well as ancient poems and ballads, carefully preserved for the Japanese people.

The tales are fanciful, candid, charming, and fearsome, as we read of two creator deities—Izanagi, meaning the Male-Who-Invites, and Izanami, the Female-Who-Invites—who came down upon the earth after the original chaos had separated into ocean and heaven. At the behest of the other gods, they created the islands and began the generation of all future inhabitants of Japan. Descending from the Floating Bridge of Heaven (i.e., a rainbow), Izanagi thrust his jeweled spear into the salty waters and the thick mud, stirred it, and then withdrew the spear, allowing the brine which dripped from its end to form an island. Izanagi and Izanami stepped down to the island and were wedded. In due time Izanami gave birth to the eight large islands of Japan.

The two deities then created thirty-five lesser gods. Kagu-Tsuchi, the heat-god, was the last to emerge from the womb. By his searing flames he killed his mother. Izanagi, outraged by the fatality, revenged himself for Izanami's death by cutting Kagu-Tsuchi into countless pieces; but he found that all the bits of Kagu-Tsuchi his swiftly slashing sword produced became more deities.

On Izanami's death she entered the Land of Yomi, the underworld. Izanagi, in sorrow and despair, followed in the hope he might induce Izanami to return to the world with him. It was too late, however; she could not go back. She was now ugly, for decomposition had set in. She begged him not to gaze upon her, but he took a comb from his hair and, lighting its end, illumined the hideous scene of her body covered with crawling maggots.

Izanami shrieked at Izanagi that he had disgraced her. She dispatched the Ugly Females of Yomi to follow after him. Izanagi fled and evaded the pursuers. Izanami then sent after him eight thunder gods which had been created in her body's decay and, in addition, ordered 1,500 warriors from Yomi to capture him. Izanagi battled them, while Izanami joined in the pursuit. When Izanagi entered the upper world, he lifted a rock mountain and with it blocked off the passage to the underworld. The two deities, now separated by both the rock and their hatred for each other, angrily said good-bye, hurling curses and epithets at each other through the wall of rock.

Izanagi, polluted and filthy, walked to the ocean's edge to bathe. He discarded his staff and his wearing apparel, whereupon each of these became a god. As he washed the corruption from his left eye, he created Amaterasu, the sun-goddess, who is the most revered of all Japanese gods. Then, by washing his right eye, he created Tsuki-yomi, the god of the moon; and by washing his nostrils he produced Susa-no-wo, the storm-god.

When, in later years, Amaterasu, the sun-goddess, gazed upon these islands from above, she was so disturbed about their problems, especially their lack of order and unity, that she decided to supplant the then ruler, son of the storm-god Susa-no-wo. She sent down from heaven her own grandson, Ni-ni-gi, with the command: "This Luxuriant-Reed-Plain-Land-of-Fresh-Rice-Ears is the land which thou shalt rule." Obeying her, Ni-ni-gi ruled on the island of Kyushu, where three generations later in 660 B.C. his great-grandson, Jimmu Tenno, became the first human emperor. He set out to conquer the province of Yamoto and establish the capital in the midst of the province of Hondo in the center of Japan's islands. The Japanese people, thinking of their emperor as in direct lineage from Amaterasu, consider themselves and their islands even now, twenty-six centuries later, to have been divine in origin, and thus they reaffirm their belief in Shinto as "the way of the gods."

The major difference between Shinto and all other major religions in the world lies in the fact that Shinto's major deity is feminine and not masculine. Another, though lesser, distinction between Shinto and other faiths is the unbroken lineage of Japan's ruling dynasty which was made possible, the Japanese have always believed, by its divine origins (it should be noted that Japan's emperor, Hirohito, disavowed his "divinity" in 1946, several months after the surrender of his country in World War II).

In its earlier centuries Shinto knew no influences other than those of Japan. Purely Japanese in its inception, it offered its devotees meaning and purpose solely in their loyalty to Japanese customs, reverence for Japanese places, and a love of the land, both in its totality and its smallest plot of ground. Their hills and mountains—such as Mount Fuji—their lakes and rivers, shrines and temples, trees and gardens had all belonged to their ancestors and were loved by them; so do they belong to and are they loved by this generation.

Although the Japanese people no longer consider Japan's divine nature to be unique among the nations of the world, it is nevertheless difficult for them to believe that Japan is not specially chosen for blessings. The gods still make their way to those beautiful shores, for to this hour most Japanese call their country "the land of the gods."

Shinto is nature worship, polytheistic to be sure but on a

higher level than in other such religions. Shinto shrines have a gateway approach (the *torii*), the upper crosspiece of which curves upward at the ends to point toward the heavens. The vista is usually upon tall cryptomeria trees or a waterfall. These sites are designed to heighten the worshipers' appreciation and reverence for nature. Shinto festivals, both plentiful and popular, pertain to the cycle of the seasons and the richness of the earth: seedtime and harvest, the full bloom of crops and fruit in fields and orchards, testing the new rice and the first products, the fullness of the moon, and the longest days of sunlight.

The shrine at Ise, dedicated to Amaterasu, is the holiest among all the shrines of Japan. Yet there are many deities almost equal with Amaterasu—not only those already mentioned but many others; the rain-god and the thunder-god, the god of lightning and the god and goddess of wind, a mountain-god and many minor mountain-gods, food and fertility deities, harbor-gods and river-gods, earthquake-gods and volcano-gods—gods almost without number, or, the Japanese say, 800 myriads of gods and goddesses. These are all called *kami,* meaning "superior" or "above."

The Japanese in earlier centuries celebrated the divine origins of their country and its people by deifying objects of any kind and natural forces of every sort. Until the fifth century A.D. a planless, haphazard old Shinto prevailed; but new trends began. In those formative years of Japan, Shinto began to take shape as certain aspects of Chinese civilization attracted the Japanese people. They altered their lives completely by learning Chinese skills and adopting more sophisticated ideas, not the least of which were the influences of Confucianism.

Hitherto, old Shinto had for the most part been tied to nature worship and an undefined ancestor worship, but now

the filial piety of Confucianists led the Japanese to a veneration of ancestors unequaled in any other country or by any
other people. The emperor had been honored by the common
people's claim of authentic direct descent for him from
Amaterasu, the sun-goddess; now not only the high officials
claimed such ancestry from gods and goddesses closely associated with her, but the lowest subjects, too, claimed at
least remote connection.

In the following century, the sixth, an even greater intellectual and spiritual force came to bear upon old Shinto, also
by way of China: Buddhism opened a new world to the
Japanese. Not only art and literature, medicine and social
service were brought to the people, but also the claim on the
part of the Buddhists that religious truth as well as the power
of determining and assorting it originated not in Japan but
rather in China and in India. The common folk proceeded to
make Buddhism their own faith because the royal family,
followed quickly by the court aristocrats, had done so.

In the eighth century a virtual merging of Shinto and
Buddhism occurred. Certain priests of Buddhism claimed
they had known visions which proved that Japan's native
gods were really Buddhas and bodhisattvas who had come
into being once again among the islands of Japan. The
Japanese called this amalgam of faiths a "two-seated" religion, meaning that their gods had been seated in Japan and
abroad, at one and the same time. Such a syncretic religion
meant that there was a "twofold way of the gods" (*Ryobu*);
Buddhist gods were "the originals," but Shinto gods were
their representation in Japan. Shinto absorbed so many
Buddhist customs and decorative motifs that it was referred
to as "two-sided Shinto" or "mixed Shinto"; and for at least
five centuries Japan was more Buddhist than Shinto, even
though the blend appeared on the surface to include both on
an equal basis.

From the thirteenth to seventeenth centuries Japanese life was in considerable confusion due in great part to the power of Buddhism, for the emperor found his royal prerogatives challenged by the Buddhist priests and his power over the military (*samurai*) and the nobility greatly diminished. A dozen generations of conflict among the feudal families came to an end around 1600; and the Tokugawas assumed control by establishing a dictator (*shogun*). The centralized control of this family, known in history as the Tokugawa regime, meant the resurgence of Shinto and its emergence from the Buddhism in which it had been almost submerged. Ryobu Shinto reversed itself; the Buddhist gods became secondary appearances, while the Japanese were the originals. Japan now shut itself off from the world, closed its seaports to foreign vessels, wiped out by ruthless extermination the Christian groups which were products of the introduction of Christianity a century earlier, and centered solely on the wisdom of the ancient Japanese. The result was "pure Shinto," a name devised to claim again descent for the emperor from the sun-goddess Amaterasu. This, the scholars of Japan maintained, was "the true ancient Way."

Pressure in the 1850s, from the Americans abetted by the Dutch, the French, and the British, finally opened the doors to Japan, first for trade and shipping facilities, then for cultural exchanges; the United States helped in this way to start and then to speed both the modernization and the industrialization of Japan. Oddly enough, the result was to imbed in the Japanese Constitution of 1889 the historic concept of the emperor's relation to Amaterasu and to give this religious claim an official sanction by the state. As a consequence, Buddhism was officially superseded; but the average person still thought and worshiped in terms of the two religions virtually in tandem.

Increasingly, however, the Japanese imperial regime continued through the late years of the nineteenth century to strengthen the newly revived national religion. It gave government support to a faith which considered the emperor to be "sacred and inviolable" and revered the empire as having been singled out by the gods, the imperial proclamation asserted, "to be reigned over and governed by a line of emperors unbroken for ages eternal."

Government-sponsored Shinto had opposition in the opening decades of the twentieth century. Of the opposing elements, the Buddhists were still striving, and protested state support for a rival cult. Another opposing factor was agnosticism, which was based on scientific methods and disciplines and held the view that no demonstrable proof is available to substantiate belief in a God or gods or in a life after death. A parallel, even stronger force was atheism, the rejection of all religious beliefs and a denial of the existence of God or the validity of religious beliefs, attitudes in great measure fostered by the popularity and seeming success of Marxism in the Soviet Union and its attractiveness for certain elements in the revolutionary ferment of nearby China.

During the 1920s and the 1930s, and in 1940–1941, just prior to Japan's entry into World War II, the government looked with favor on the efforts of Japanese scholars to reconcile the ancient Shinto with modern science and still retain in the national patriotism the view that their deities (*kami*) were uniquely their own, whether in the heavens above or the earth beneath, whether in the solitude and beauty of thousands of shrines or in nature itself. Whatever inspired awe and reverence, whether in solemn ceremonies or in impressive landscapes, contained the divine.

Japanese governments from the 1880s down through World War I fostered the state-supported Shinto (Jinja-Shinto), as distinguished from a sectarian Shinto (Kyoha-

Shinto). State Shinto was designed to center attention on a national morality, a way of the gods which venerated forefathers and acknowledged its legacy from imperial ancestors. Only through "the sentiment of reverence," the government documents asserted, could men foster "the feeling of respect for ancestors" and establish "the foundations of the national morality."

State shrines, numbering at one time more than a hundred thousand, were considered more as national and patriotic centers than as specifically religious sanctuaries. Yet the line of demarcation was hard to draw between the two. The emperor was accustomed to appear at the Grand Imperial Shrine of Ise when he ascended the throne or when the nation declared war. Usually, through representatives and messengers, the emperor sent both offerings and reports of national significance; in addition, the emperor took part in the ritual of purification (*o-harai*) which absolved the nation's wrongdoings and shortcomings through the intercession of priests at Ise and other state shrines in Japan.

Through the centuries the Japanese paired the way of the gods with the way of their warriors. The military officer caste, the samurai, practiced a warrior's code known as *bushido*. For centuries this Way of the Warrior-Knight prevailed in Japan, although as a set of rules it lacked specific stipulations and requirements. Bushido was an ideal, a spirit, a mode of military etiquette, a warrior's conduct. Some trace its power to the ethical rigor of Confucianism, and its flawless discipline of the self to Zen Buddhism, but the centuries-old feudalism of Japan developed the absolute obedience to a superior and a code of honor which must not be altered or compromised. Shinto unified all three of these contributions —and doubtless many more from ancient days. By the fervor of patriotism, Shinto fused them into one, demanding an uncritical loyalty to the emperor primarily, and to the nation and to feudal chieftains secondarily.

The code of bushido called for such loyalty, but it also expected gratitude for the gift of life as well as courage in the living of it and, if at all possible, in the giving of it on behalf of a warrior's feudal lord. It elicited unselfishness, especially in the performance of duty; utter truthfulness; politeness, even to an enemy; reticence, particularly in hiding one's emotions; and the primacy of honor which caused a warrior to prefer death to disgrace and implied unquestioning willingness to commit suicide by the age-old ceremony of *harakiri* (self-disembowelment).

The bushido code determined the conduct of Japanese soldiers and civilians not only in feudal times but in more recent generations as well. Until 1945, the end of World War II, Shinto priests presided at special rituals before certain altars on a chosen memorial day so that the people might honor the spirits of their hero dead. By such rites the living could invite the souls of these departed soldiers to return for the respect, honor, and gratitude of their kinsfolk and countrymen.

Shinto called for the utmost in patriotism, a nationalism raised to the intensity of religion. This fusion of religion, nationalism, and militarism, sanctioned by the support of the state, led the Japanese people to believe that their destiny was to carry Japanese conquest and power throughout Asia, and eventually the whole world. The surrender of Japan in August 1945 brought an end to that delusion.

After the war, state Shinto no longer had government aid or encouragement, for American occupation authorities canceled such support. The effect, while momentarily disruptive, was eventually healthy. Voluntary support took the place of government subsidy; and a more authentic devotion, uncomplicated by public pressures, developed in its stead. Despite the disestablishment of state Shinto, shrines throughout the land retain the traditional emblems of the emperor's divinity—namely, the mirror, the sword, and the jewel which hang upon the simple, otherwise unadorned, walls. The mirror symbolizes sincerity, guilelessness, and wisdom; the sword denotes courage; the jewel represents benevolence and generosity.

The practice of Shinto in the home has became stronger. Many homes have their own private shrine (*miya*) which honors ancestors and has sacred objects on a god-shelf (*kami-dana*). Before this shrine the simplest oblation of the day, an expression of gratitude or an offering of food, is placed, and more elaborate ceremonies, celebrating birth and marriage and death, are observed. The reverence for nature and the belief in bodily cleanliness remain integral parts of Shinto, but a blind loyalty to the nation and unquestioning obedience to its patriotic demands are no longer expected. There is not now in Shinto, as there never has been, an inner life of religious devotion, so characteristic of other religions in Eastern lands; nor is there any striving after outward objectives of justice and equity in society.

The Buddhist customs, especially those concerning the farewell to the dead, still intrude on Shinto; and many a home in Japan is graced not only by the god-shelf, the *kami-dana,* but also a Buddha-shelf, the *butsu-dana.* Buddhism is no longer so powerful in Japan, but claims the adherence of at least one half (some authorities estimate two thirds) of the Japanese people.

Although Shinto enjoys coexistence with Buddhism, as well as with Confucianism, Taoism, and Christianity, it has a basic national flavor and quality which are indigenous to Japan and therefore appeal to the Japanese people, molding many of their habits and coloring their culture. Some observers maintain, however, that Shinto in particular, and these other traditional faiths in general, encounter a casual, often indifferent reaction from the average Japanese. Judgments of this sort are easy to make but hard to substantiate; yet it is clear that a sifting of evidence and a rethinking of attitudes are going on today, and Shinto cannot remain unaffected.

Shinto in its non-state form has spawned a large number of sects, too numerous to count and too disparate to describe in detail. During the years immediately after World War II these sects proliferated in number and variety, some of a nature wholly foreign to their Shinto origin.

In addition, Shinto is flanked by a wide variety of new religions in Japan, ranging from faith healing to an optimistic monotheism; most of them are born of the anxieties and the stresses of a nation thrust by rapid industrialization and modernization into new responsibilities. Shinto is challenged, and some say even threatened, by these new-found faiths which abound in modern Japan.

The Japanese justify this maze of groups and ideas, this host of deities and practices, by quoting a favorite proverb of their land: "Even though you should worship but one God, yet all the other gods will be pleased."

PART TWO

From the Middle East

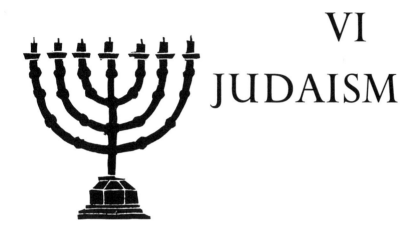

VI
JUDAISM

People of the Covenant

THE COVENANT, a solemn and binding agreement, was
the promise made by God to the Jews on many occasions, but primarily to Abraham and Moses, central
figures in the rise of Judaism and key characters in the drama
of the Jewish people. Exactly what the words and clauses
of the compact were no man knows. Yet men do know that
Abraham of the twentieth and nineteenth centuries B.C. felt
impelled to lead his flocks and kinsmen to a new life in other
lands; and Moses, of a later day, amid harassment and un-
certainties interpreted to the people of Israel the commandments given him by Yahweh, awesome and feared and
honored god of the Hebrews, soon to become for them the
One God, the "I Am Who I Am." (The word appears in
the Hebrew Bible as YHWH. By inserting vowel sounds

between the consonants *y, h,* and *w* or *v,* it was pronounced "Yahweh" and was to be uttered only once a year by the High Priest in the Holy of Holies; later, Christian translators of the Bible incorrectly rendered the name as Jehovah.)

An unknown number of centuries of religious development preceded these two towering figures, Abraham and Moses, who were separated by at least 400 (and perhaps as much as 900) years. The Hebrews seem to have come from Semitic tribes stemming from the northern reaches of the deserts of Arabia. For hundreds of years they had lived as nomads in those bleak, treeless and arid plains. Led by their ruling elders, the patriarchs, these wanderers had banded together to protect themselves against the forces of nature, which were often hostile and destructive, and to defend themselves against any intruders.

Like countless other tribes in the second and third millennia B.C., the ancient Hebrews had a religion of thoroughgoing animism: they venerated pillars and stones and rocks and hills, believing them to be alive and to be the abode of spirits, whether divine or devilish. Grateful for water, they looked upon oases (few and remote) as having special powers; they feared that if they vexed their gods, then the springs, brooks, and cisterns would dry up. The gods, whether of water or of foliage, had to be appeased; trees knew a divine strength, as the rarity of holy groves in the desert had proven, but as the hiding place for wild animals, a demonic revenge as well. Birds, reptiles, and animals possessed devils' powers, whether as eagles or serpents, leopards or foxes. The winds, especially when thrust by tornadoes of the desert or inflamed by the relentless sun, bore evil; yet winds could be gentle and kind, and for these the gods should be thanked.

From such varied and many powers came the Hebrew

word *elohim* which was the plural of *el,* a divinity; as in
other religions, the gods were thought of as names for and
as attributes of the One True God. Eventually *elohim* came
to refer to the Supreme Power and the Divine Reality hundreds of millions across the centuries have called God.

The shift from animism and polytheism toward monotheism, the belief in one God for which the Jewish people
are justly famed, was long and tortuous. In the process, the
god and gods of the Hebrews became a God who had a
unique relationship with His people, something more than a
king to his subjects or a father to his son. Yahweh was no
longer one deity among many; now he was the sole deity
because He had "chosen" His children—or subjects or
sons—and had an out-of-the-ordinary tie to them in a
covenant. This contract or compact bound both Him and
His people by an indissoluble bond.

The man who sensed this relationship, almost as acutely
and dynamically as Moses would later, was Abraham,
the only figure in Hebrew history before Moses who is in
any way comparable to him, or can be said to have rivaled
him. A number of centuries before Moses—probably about
the twentieth or nineteenth century B.C.—this partially
mythical and partially genuine patriarch lived near the great
city of Ur in Chaldea, a part of Babylonia in a region of
southwestern Asia adjacent to the Euphrates River and the
Persian Gulf. Either as a legendary character or an authentic
personality of history, Abraham took his tribe westward and
southward through the lands we know today as Syria,
Jordan, and Israel. Their destination was the fertile region
around the Nile in Egypt. Their motivation was security
from hunger and attack, and their objective, freedom from
encroachment and onslaughts by swarms of other migrating
peoples. Many of these invading tribes were the same Indo-

Europeans and Aryans who played important roles in the rise of the religions discussed in earlier chapters. Abraham led the Hebrews, or "Habiru," and relied on one deity alone, a god of the mountains known as El-Shaddai.

Encouraged by El-Shaddai, Abraham set out for the safety and verdure he and his flocks and herds and tribesmen craved. As his chroniclers in future centuries told the story in the first book of the Bible, Genesis: "Now the Lord said unto Abram [i.e., Abraham]: 'Get thee out of thy country, and from thy kindred, and from thy father's house, unto the land that I will show thee.' "

Abraham was assured: " 'And I will make of thee a great nation, and I will bless thee, and make thy name great; and be thou a blessing.' "

He was not afraid, for he had the promise of his God: " 'And I will bless them that bless thee, and him that curseth thee will I curse; and in thee shall all the families of the earth be blessed.' "

Abraham and his followers came down the eastern coast of the Mediterranean to the Levant, the eastern shore of the Mediterranean Sea, a land where a people called Canaanites lived. There they settled for an indeterminate time.

When Abraham was "ninety years old and nine," the covenant between God and this doughty, picturesque nomad was reaffirmed:

"I am God Almighty; walk before Me, and be thou wholehearted. . . . And I will make My covenant between Me and thee, and will multiply thee exceedingly. . . . As for Me, behold, My covenant is with thee, and thou shalt be the father of a multitude of nations. . . . And I will make thee exceeding fruitful, and I will make nations of thee, and kings shall come out of thee. And I will establish My covenant between Me and thee and thy seed after thee throughout their generations for an everlasting covenant, to be a God unto thee and to thy seed after thee. And I will give unto thee, and to thy seed after thee, the land of thy sojournings, all the land of Canaan, for an everlasting possession; and I will be their God. . . . And as for thee, thou shalt keep My covenant, thou, and thy seed after thee throughout their generations."

Abraham's descendants lived in the Levant with their families and flocks and prospered; but when a devastating famine struck, they moved to the border of Egypt. The stories of the succeeding generations—Isaac and Jacob and Joseph—are told in moving fashion in Genesis. Again the Hebrews migrated, this time transferred by the conquering Pharaoh to Egypt itself; by the sixteenth century B.C., they had become bonded slaves. For what appears in historical records to have been two to three centuries longer, the enslaved Hebrews toiled for the Pharaohs of Egypt, undoubtedly in the building of pyramids.

From their midst in the late fourteenth century B.C. came Moses, heroic figure of Hebrew destiny. Adopted by the daughter of Pharaoh, he was reared at the imperial court where he grew to manhood. When he saw an Egyptian beat one of his fellow Hebrews, he killed the Egyptian; then he fled to Midian where he married and settled. Later, to the Jews—and by a newly named God—the Covenant stood as described in the Book of Exodus:

And the angel of the Lord appeared unto him [Moses] in a flame of fire out of the midst of a bush; and he looked, and, behold, the bush burned with fire, and the bush was not consumed. . . . God called unto him out

of the midst of the bush, and said: "Moses, Moses."
And he said: "Here am I." And He said: "Draw not
nigh hither; put off thy shoes from off thy feet, for the
place whereon thou standest is holy ground. . . . I am
the God of thy father, the God of Abraham, the God of
Isaac, and the God of Jacob."

Then Moses asked, "Behold, when I come unto the children of Israel, and shall say unto them: The God of your
fathers hath sent me unto you; and they shall say to me:
What is His name? what shall I say unto them?"

The answer came: "I AM THAT I AM [*ehyeh asher
ehyeh*]. . . . Thus shalt thou say unto the children of
Israel: I AM [*ehyeh,* which sounds not unlike Yahweh]
hath sent me unto you."

Appointed by this God, Yahweh (formerly known as
El-Shaddai), Moses accepted his commission to lead the
children of Israel out of bondage. The tale, told in dramatic
detail in Exodus and Numbers, is one of the most familiar
narratives in all literature. The highlight is the confrontation
on Mount Sinai when Yahweh gives Moses two tablets of
stone and, in the Ten Commandments inscribed on them,
reasserts the Covenant:

> "I am the Lord thy God, Who brought thee out of the
> land of Egypt, out of the house of bondage.
>
> "Thou shalt have no other gods before Me. Thou
> shalt not make unto thee a graven image, nor any manner
> of likeness, of any thing that is in heaven above, or that is
> in the earth beneath, or that is in the water under the
> earth; thou shalt not bow down unto them, nor serve
> them; for I the Lord thy God am a jealous God, visiting
> the iniquity of the fathers upon the children unto the
> third and fourth generation of them that hate Me; and

showing mercy unto the thousandth generation of them that love Me and keep My commandments.

"Thou shalt not take the name of the Lord thy God in vain; for the Lord will not hold him guiltless that taketh His name in vain.

"Remember the sabbath day, to keep it holy. Six days shalt thou labor, and do all thy work; but the seventh day is a sabbath unto the Lord thy God, in it thou shalt not do any manner of work, thou, nor thy son, nor thy daughter, nor thy man-servant, nor thy maid-servant, nor thy cattle, nor thy stranger that is within thy gates; for in six days the Lord made heaven and earth, the sea, and all that in them is, and rested on the seventh day; wherefore the Lord blessed the sabbath day, and hallowed it.

"Honor thy father and thy mother, that thy days may be long upon the land which the Lord thy God giveth thee.

"Thou shalt not murder.

"Thou shalt not commit adultery.

"Thou shalt not steal.

"Thou shalt not bear false witness against thy neighbor.

"Thou shalt not covet thy neighbor's house; thou shalt not covet thy neighbor's wife, nor his man-servant, nor his maid-servant, nor his ox, nor his ass, nor any thing that is thy neighbor's."

For forty years Moses was the leader of his people as they moved on toward their Promised Land of Canaan, but his death occurred just before the entry into Canaan. His successor, Joshua, led the Hebrews in their battles and finally subjugated the hostile tribes.

Now began the long process of refining the religion of

Yahweh and resisting the nature worship of the Canaanites and their *baalim*—nature gods and goddesses represented by Baal and the goddess Astarte. During the time of the "Judges," the twelfth through tenth centuries B.C., the worship of Yahweh included reverence for powers which had belonged to the Baal-Astarte worship; and the Hebrew prophets assumed the difficult task of purifying the Yahweh worship.

The earlier prophets—of the eleventh and tenth centuries B.C.—included soothsayers and ecstatic men who were prone to superstition. They were replaced by more rationalistic men—Nathan during the reign of King David, Ahijah in the years of King Solomon's rule, Elijah in the time of King Ahab, and Elijah's successor, Elisha. They felt impelled to speak the truth, bluntly and unequivocally. Each contributed to the growing realization among the Israelites that their God, Yahweh, was superior to Baal; but the struggle to convince all the people took centuries.

In the eighth and seventh centuries B.C. came a procession of great men, who took seriously their role as prophets—men who spoke on behalf of God. Each one of this lively and heterogeneous but utterly courageous group of men made his own unique contribution.

Amos, often called the prophet of righteousness, cried out as Yahweh's spokesman: ". . . Let justice well up as waters, and righteousness as a mighty stream." This he contrasted with Yahweh's saying, "I hate, I despise your feasts, and I will take no delight in your solemn assemblies."

Hosea, termed by many the prophet of grace, spoke of God's forgiving love:

"I will heal their backsliding,
I will love them freely;
For Mine anger is turned away. . . ."

Isaiah announced a divine imperative: "And I heard the voice of the Lord, saying: 'Whom shall I send, and who will go for us?' Then I said: 'Here am I; send me.' " As a prophet of social justice, he warned of a Day of Doom awaiting the evildoer and the faithless, the exploiters and the heartless: "Woe unto them that join house to house, that lay field to field, till there be no room, and ye be made to dwell alone in the midst of the land! . . . . Seek justice, relieve the oppressed, judge the fatherless, plead for the widow."

A second Isaiah, usually called the unknown prophet of the exile in Babylon, is remembered from his eloquent writings in chapters 40 to 66 of the bibical book of Isaiah; he described God as the One and Only, for "there is no other":

Hast thou not known? hast thou not heard
That the everlasting God, the Lord,
The Creator of the ends of the earth,
Fainteth not, neither is weary?

He spoke of, or is thought to have spoken of, the coming of a messiah, "the Suffering Servant of Israel."

Micah, though a spokesman for justice among men and pleader for peace on earth, inveighed against formalism and ritualism in religion. Much more concerned about social behavior than the methods of worship, he spoke words which, though worldwide repetition for almost 2700 years has made them famous and familiar, are never trite or outworn:

Wherewith shall I come before the Lord,
And bow myself before God on high?
Shall I come before Him with burnt-offerings,
With calves of a year old?
Will the Lord be pleased with thousands of rams,

With ten thousands of rivers of oil?
Shall I give my first-born for my transgression,
The fruit of my body for the sin of my soul?
It hath been told thee, O man, what is good,
And what the Lord doth require of thee:
Only to do justly, and to love mercy, and to walk
   humbly with thy God.

Jeremiah, a prophet of both personal religion and social justice, cared less for Jerusalem and the temple than he did for a renewed Covenant with God. In contrast, Ezekiel, a priestly prophet, emphasized purity of worship by evoking visions, enunciating allegories, and presenting a new code of observances for the temple.

In substance, these literary prophets had concern for the community and bespoke the dignity of man, giving renewed emphasis to the commands in the book of Leviticus: "Thou shalt love thy neighbor as thyself" and "thou shalt be kind to the stranger within thy gates. . . . If a stranger sojourn with thee in your land, ye shall not do him wrong. The stranger that sojourneth with you shall be unto you as the home-born among you, and thou shalt love him as thyself; for ye were strangers in the land of Egypt. . . ."

These stalwarts, holding forth hope for the future and underscoring the unique mission of the people of Israel, called for a return to a purer worship of Yahweh and a more righteous life for both the individual and society. They were emulated by less well known but equally redoubtable men like Habakkuk of 600 B.C. who preached that "the just shall live by his faith"; the sensitive, aristocratic Zephaniah of an earlier generation, who was so morally earnest and warned against sin's punishment on the "Day of the Lord"; the anonymous eighth century B.C. author of the book of

Jonah who preferred universalism to exclusiveness and preached of God's redemption; Nahum, poet and patriot of the seventh century B.C., who predicted retribution for the evildoer; and Joel of the fourth century B.C., who prophesied—with both vividness and accuracy—that plagues of locusts would bring disaster, but held out against pessimism and shared his high hopes for a better day:

And it shall come to pass afterward,
That I will pour out My spirit upon all flesh:
And your sons and your daughters shall prophesy,
Your old men shall dream dreams,
Your young men shall see visions. . . .

All underscored the need for a proper relationship with Yahweh, God of righteousness and justice. These prophets are unique among religionists of any era; and the major prophets among them—Isaiah and the second Isaiah, Jeremiah and Ezekiel, Amos, Hosea, and Micah—must be included among the religious geniuses of history.

By this time their beliefs and teachings had crystallized into a more permanent pattern, a set way of life which was different in emphasis from the peoples' cultures and religions in surrounding lands. The Hebrews had set human value and human dignity in opposition to slavery and injustice: " 'Not by power nor by might, but by My spirit,' saith the Lord God of Hosts."

Through the next two and a half millennia the people of Israel in their many wanderings continued to cherish this covenant with their God, a God of all mankind, it was true, but tied first and foremost to them. They remembered this bond in the destruction of their temple in 586 B.C. by Nebuchadnezzar and as well during its restoration by Cyrus the Great in 538 B.C. They relied on it in their encounter with the influence of Greece after Alexander the Great's conquests in the Levant and in resistance to many aspects of Hellenic culture during the fourth and third centuries; then later in rebellion against Roman power. During the destruction of the temple by Titus in A.D. 70 and in their dispersion for nineteen centuries thereafter in more than a hundred different countries, the Jews harked back to their Covenant.

A longing for restoration to their national homeland lay deep in their hearts and echoed in spoken prayers on their lips; the yearning to rebuild the lost temple never left their thoughts and prayers. Oppressed everywhere, the Jews cherished their hope for restoration of the temple and self-determination in their ancient land in conformance with Mosaic law. Their struggles to survive amid persecution— whether by the Moslems after the Islamic conquests, the Christian Crusaders, the Spaniards of the Inquisition, or the Hitlerite Germans and the Soviets of the twentieth century —were fired by a hope: they would be rescued and justice would ultimately be done.

This hope and this faith were buttressed by their Torah (Pentateuch, the biblical books of the Law of Moses), reinforced and reinterpreted by the prophets and by such scholars as Hillel of first-century A.D. Palestine and Moses Maimonides of twelfth-century Spain and Egypt. Jewish love of learning, hailed in Jewish annals for a thousand years and more before the Christian Era, came to flower again in the formation of the Talmud, the gathering of every definition and descriptive account of Jewish beliefs and practices whether in the written law of the Pentateuch, the "oral" rabbinic law of the Halakah, or the sermonic and often folkloristic interpretations by rabbis through many centuries in the Midrash.

The Talmud has two main parts: one, the Mishnah,

which grew up in Palestine, brought together the precepts
of early rabbinical law, interpreted the Torah, and in beautiful Hebrew kept alive a rare collection of brief, concise
aphorisms; and two, the Gemara, which developed largely
in Babylon after the destruction of the Temple in A.D. 70
but to some extent also in Jerusalem, during the bleak centuries of national homelessness, and is the elaboration of the
Mishnah. This vast work gave rise in later centuries to an
even larger body of commentaries by famous, learned rabbis
in Talmudic schools and synagogues in scores of lands
through many hundreds of years.

Two examples of the Talmudic writings reflect a pithy,
provocative quality. The first illustrates the Hebraic form of
the Golden Rule (as in many other religions, in negative
form):

> A certain heathen came to Shammai and said to him:
> Convert me provided that you teach me the entire Torah
>   while I stand on one foot.
> Shammai drove him away with the builder's cubit which
>   was in his hand.
> He went to Hillel who said to him:
> What is hateful to you, do not do to your neighbor:
> that is the entire Torah;
> the rest is commentary;
> go and learn it.

The other instance points to the universal aspects of Judaism, giving the lie to assertions of uninformed people that
Judaism is bent on exclusive, parochial requirements:

> Whence do we know that even a Gentile who engages in
>   the Torah is like a high priest?
> We learn it from: "Ye shall therefore keep My statutes,

and Mine ordinances, which if a man do, he shall live
by them" (Lev. 18:5)
"Priests, Levites, and Israelites," was not said, but "a
man";
thus you may learn that even a Gentile who engages in
the Torah—
lo, he is like a high priest.

These brief examples reflect a whole philosophy in a few
words. There are countless other such quotations equally
picturesque and pertinent. All, basic to Judaism, reflect the
Jews' conviction that deeds and conduct are decisive factors
in life; and they illustrate the fact that salvation is open to
all, Jew and Gentile alike.

In these several collections, the Jews succeeded in gathering every item of learning within their entity as the Jewish
people, the framework of Jewish culture, and the structure
of their religion, Judaism. Here in the Talmud and its
commentaries, and also in the splendid, expressive liturgy
the Jews created, was a bulwark of resistance to tyranny and
persecution that has sustained them for nearly two thousand
years. The Covenant with Yahweh, now in truth the God
of Abraham, Isaac, and Jacob, had been maintained and
would continue to be maintained by the Jewish people.

When Christians and Moslems, the former at the beginning of the so-called Christian Era and the latter from the
sixth and seventh centuries, sought to convert Jews, their
rejection of conversion was adamant. The Jews refused to
look upon Jesus as the Christ, the Messiah, whether they
were entreated by Paul (formerly the rabbinic disciple, Saul
of Tarsus), the eloquence of the Church Fathers, or the
persuasive arguments of medieval philosophers of the Christian church; moreover, the persecution and discrimination

the Jews experienced at the hands of Christians were not conducive to conversion—in fact, just the opposite.

The forces of Islam tended at first to be more open-minded, kindly, and tolerant than the Christians. Under Islamic rule a creative revival of Jewish faith, practice, and learning took place, especially in Spain and North Africa during the eleventh and twelfth centuries, and was furthered by the philosophers Maimonides (1135–1204) and Nahmanides (1194–1270). By the eleventh century, however, Moslem oppression of the Jew had already begun.

The Christians' expulsion of the Jews during the centuries of the Crusades—first from parts of Germany; then, in 1290, from England; from France in 1394; and finally, in 1492, from Spain—drove them partly to the Middle East, to Syria and Turkey, but also to Italy and, in great numbers, to Poland, where a welcome awaited them but integration with the indigenous population was impossible. In Eastern Europe and in the ghettos of Germany and Austria, a language known as Yiddish, a combination of low German dialect and words borrowed from the language of the country in which the Jews happened then to live, a jargon always written in Hebrew characters, began to develop and to create a rich Yiddish culture.

Even before these many centuries of enforced exile and the periodic but brief returns to the Holy Land which the Jews still thought of as their Promised Land, they had developed a number of dramatic, stirring festivals and fasting times to heighten the meaning of their religious practices. Pesach or Passover, the festival of freedom, referred to the time of the Exodus, their redemption from Egyptian slavery, and was linked with the coming of springtime; the Seder, a ritual meal on the first evening of Passover, centered around the eating of unleavened bread during the entire week, the drinking of four cups of wine, and eating bitter herbs and roots and parsley, dipped in salt water, as a reminder of suffering in previous centuries. These reminded the participants of Jewish ordeals in the days of captivity, and at the Seder, the *Haggadah,* or "Narration," retold the whole story, with part of it in question-and-answer form. After the singing of Psalms, the repeating of prayers, and relating the story of the Exodus, the door was opened, partly to symbolize that all hungry passers-by were to be admitted, partly to show that nothing was concealed and, to refute the hoary charges of ritual murder, to prove that no child had been killed, but mostly to enable the spirit of Elijah, forerunner of the Messiah, to come in and drink from the Elijah Cup, standing ready for him on the Seder table during the ceremony.

Fifty days after the Seder, Jews observe Shavuot, the Feast of Weeks, to give thanks for the Law that had been given on Mount Sinai in that season of the year and to rejoice over the first fruits of the spring harvest of wheat.

In the early autumn, they celebrate Rosh Hashanah, their religious New Year's Day. This day is noted in the Talmud as a "Day of Judgment" and is observed by the blowing of the shofar, the ram's horn, which summons the listeners to the synagogue that they may reassess their lives, think about their actions in the past, recall their Creator, and come to Him in contrition and repentance.

Dovetailed with this holiday are the subsequent ten days of repentance. At the conclusion comes the observance of Yom Kippur, the great Day of Atonement, when the people fast in complete abstinence from all food and drink for twenty-four hours—from just before the previous night's worship service to the following evening when the stars appear. The "Kol Nidre," the atonement prayer chanted in a traditional melody on the eve of Yom Kippur, grants absolution from the sin of unkept vows. Each worshiper is expected to turn away from evildoing and to atone for the wrongs he has done during the past year, promising to fulfill the will of God from this time forward.

Five days later is the observance of the thanksgiving-harvest of Sukkot, the Feast of Tabernacles or Booths, when for eight days the observants take their meals in a tabernacle or booth decorated with flowers and fruit and hold in prayer branches of the myrtle, the willow, and the palm along with the citron fruit, all symbols reminiscent of the Land of Israel and its grain and grapes, fruits of the fields and of the vine, and God's providence.

To conclude these holy days comes Simkhath Torah, the day when Jews rejoice in the Law. The sacred scrolls of the Pentateuch are taken from the Ark of the synagogue to be carried in solemn, yet joyous, procession through the aisles of the house of worship. The reading of the Pentateuch is ended for the year, for it has been the practice to read a portion every Sabbath in the services; and then the cycle of readings is immediately begun again, to be continued for another year.

In recent decades two ancient festivals of the winter season have become increasingly popular. One is Hanukkah, the "Feast of Lights," when, through a period of eight days, candles are lighted each night in synagogue and home—one on the first night alongside a special candle, or oil, reserved to light all others, and additional ones on subsequent nights, until all eight have been lighted to fill the Menorah, the festival candelabrum; these candles recall the recapture of Jerusalem and the rededication of the temple in 165 B.C. by Judas Maccabeus. The second feast is Purim, the "Feast of Lots," observed in February or March, four weeks before

Passover, and associated with the Book of Esther in the Bible, which relates Queen Esther's successful efforts to rescue her fellow Jews from abuse and persecution in Persia. A carnival atmosphere—something like Mardi Gras—with singing and dancing in the homes of the people, prevails for the entire day of Purim; gifts are sent to poor people, while members of the family and close friends exchange gifts. Hanukkah and Purim are more secular festivals and have strong nationalistic overtones, the former with its reference to the Maccabees and the latter with its retelling of the story of Esther.

In more recent generations, there have arisen within Judaism departures from strict traditionalism: Conservative Judaism, a modified though still tradition-oriented American development of the late nineteenth century; and Reform Judaism, the product of nineteenth-century religious liberals from Germany, Great Britain, and, above all, the United States.

Judaism has also suffered bitter attacks, first from rationalists who sought to discredit it, and second from Marxists who maintained that religion is "the opiate of the people." Third—and certainly worst of all—was the attack of the Nazis under the maniacal impetus of Adolf Hitler. The Nazis tried to root out Judaism because it was the fount of basic values in the Western civilization Hitler scorned and vilified, and they sought to exterminate the Jewish people itself. Hitler had a psychotic hatred for the Jews. The concepts of political liberalism and democracy he abhorred had come in part from the Jews and Judaism; and, in his mania for dictatorship (*Fuehrer Prinzip*), he vowed their annihilation. In addition, he used against the Jews all the malevolent lies which anti-Semites had perpetrated during the preceding 1,900 years of Jewish homelessness. Though the slaughter of more than six million Jews in Nazi death camps aroused the unavailing protests of many Jews and all too few Christians, the extermination of Jews continued unabated until the end of World War II in Europe.

More than one third of all the Jewish people were killed by the Nazis; but from the carnage came a creative event in the history of the Jews, namely the establishment of a Hebrew-speaking, Jewish state, Israel, the third Jewish commonwealth. Here was the fulfillment of the national hope which had lain dormant across nineteen centuries but had always been present in the prayer, "Next year in Jerusalem!"

The new state of Israel was a result of the Zionist movement, mostly inarticulate and unorganized before 1897 but increasingly articulate and organized after Dr. Theodor Herzl, author of *The Jewish State,* convened the First Zionist Congress at Basle in that year. This impressive movement continued through the first half of the twentieth century and became quite significant in great Jewish communities like those of Eastern Europe and the Americas, as well as in Palestine itself. In the three years following World War II, pressures of immigration from displaced persons in Europe and North Africa combined with the fact of Jewish settlement in Palestine, agitation by American Jews, and the power of an awakened conscience of the nations, aware at last of their complicity, through silence and inaction, in Hitler's holocaust, to help found the new state of Israel.

Even after these two decades of Israel's existence as an independent state, it is still too soon to judge its impact on Judaism. Hebrew has, during the last three quarters of a century, been reborn as a modern language, but a complex set of circumstances in Israel makes it risky to foretell what the new state will mean religiously and what lies in store generally for the religious aspirations of the Jewish people all over the world. In Israel, a religious bloc of three Orthodox political parties tries—with considerable success—to place severe restrictions upon those Jews who would prefer not to observe some of the traditional practices and rituals of Judaism, including, for example, the kosher food laws and strict Sabbath observance. Orthodox, or traditional, Judaism, as it has been known over many centuries and as it is practiced in a number of nations throughout the world, is influential enough in Israel to secure unrestricted freedom for itself there. The practice of Conservative and Reform Judaism is hindered by the Orthodox in Israel; but this situation may not last very much longer. Most Israeli Jews seem indifferent to strict Orthodoxy, and it is only to avoid disrupting the unity of Israeli society that they tolerate the authority of their country's Orthodox rabbinate. One day their patience will probably disappear and so will the control which the Orthodox now possess over the religious life of Israel. Such a transition seems to be under way.

Judaism, at this juncture, proves that the Jewish people has survived because of a sense of oneness, an ethnic consciousness, and a religiosity kept aglow by the heritage of the Covenant. Jews have succeeded in reviving their own religion—not only in rethinking rituals and symbols of the past but in recapturing the meaning of prophetic faith—by critically appraising the social order and refurbishing ethical concepts in spiritual ideals from the past. The leading Jewish communities of today are those of North America, Israel, Great Britain, France, and Argentina. The Jews of the Soviet Union are the second largest Jewish community in the world, but they suffer under severe restrictions.

Partly due to the discovery in 1947 of the Dead Sea Scrolls—commonly called the Qumran Scrolls because of their discovery by a shepherd boy in caves near Qumran on the Dead Sea—there have emerged an increased interest in the Hebrew Bible and a reinforcement of belief in the essential historicity of the biblical narrative. Archaeological research and exploration in modern Israel, as well as in the surrounding lands, have resulted in a fresh interest in the origins of Judaism. There is worldwide interest in the work of such archaeologists as Nelson Glueck, President of the Hebrew Union College-Jewish Institute of Religion, such as his discovery of King Solomon's copper mines and Ezion-Gaber: Elath. His identification of the towns and irrigation projects of the forgotten Nabatean civilization has called much attention to the Negev, Israel's southern wilderness.

The recent invitation of General Yigael Yadin, professor of archaeology at the Hebrew University in Jerusalem, to amateur archaeologists from all over the world, to help him excavate the ruins of the ancient fortress on the flat rock plateau atop Masada near the Dead Sea, resulted in a flood of acceptances. There ensued from 1963 to 1965 a swift, dramatic uncovering of both remarkable artifacts and ancient scrolls in this mountain fastness where in 73 A.D. 960 Jewish Zealots chose death rather than submit to the Romans. When the young Israelis, on three different occasions each year, take their newest recruits in the army to the top of Masada and vow, "Masada shall not fall again!", something of the vitality and the tenacity of Judaism, something of the lasting strength of this monotheistic faith from ancient Ur of the Chaldees and Mount Sinai are highlighted for our own age. The Jews of the modern world—descendants of the Patriarchs and the Judges, the Prophets and the Talmudists—still repeat their ancient chant: "Hear, O Israel, the Lord thy God is One."

VII
CHRISTIANITY

The Greatest of
These Is Love

NO LIVING RELIGION in today's world focuses so clearly and unequivocally on a single man as does Christianity. In Jesus of Nazareth, as both founder of the faith and the incarnation of God, Christianity centers all its meaning and all its allegiance—on his birth, the words and deeds of his active life, the drama of his death and resurrection.

The Gospels of the New Testament in the Bible (Mark, Matthew, Luke, and John in the order they were written) tell the story of this unique person. The Book of Acts describes the first days of the early Christian movement and its expansion throughout the Mediterranean world. The Epistles convey the essential elements of the thought and aspiration of the first generations of Christians.

Palestine, the homeland of Jesus' people, the Jews, was

under Roman rule, an oppressive authority which was both
resented and resisted by the indigenous Jews. But they did
not present a united front, and their community was
splintered into many opposing factions. Conflict among contending groups of Jews was intense in an atmosphere of
clashing religious ideas.

Among these groups, of which we know at least seven by
name, two were outstanding, the Pharisees and the Sadducees. Both were intensely committed to the Law as recorded in the first five books of the Bible (the Torah). But
the Pharisees were primarily devoted to personal righteousness, to be attained by rigorous conformity to a complicated
array of detailed regulations and ceremonies, living every
moment under the rules and precepts of religious observance.
The Sadducees, with doctrinal differences from these pie-
tists, were more worldly in temper and more nationalistic in
policy; they constituted a stricter, though rather less democratic sect which accepted the Torah but rejected Pharisaic
notions like resurrection and immortality, the oral tradition
in the Law, and the existence of angels and demons. The
Sadducees wanted to retain the *status quo* in politics and religion alike. Another sect was the Essenes, who expected the
immediate coming of the messiah; they opposed slavery and
economic exchange and advocated communal ownership of
goods, they also abstained from marital relations and insisted
on cleanliness, white garments, ceremonial purity, and strict
observance of the Sabbath day.

It was into a Jewish community deeply divided by these
political and religious factions that Jesus was born. The place
of his birth was reportedly Bethlehem, a town in Judea a
few miles south of Jerusalem, while his parents, Mary and
Joseph, were visiting there. The year was not the year one
of what has come to be known as the Christian Era; it was

probably four or six years before that. The incorrect date was set many centuries later by a monk who made a miscalculation.

Jesus grew to manhood in Nazareth, a town of Galilee. He followed in youth the family trade, carpentry. From Luke's story of Jesus, at the age of twelve, lingering in the temple long after his parents had begun the return journey to Nazareth and sitting "in the midst of the doctors, both hearing them and asking them questions," it appears that even as a child Jesus was immersed in religious inquiry and interpretation. All his days he had a sage's mind and a poet's sensitivity with a rare gift for putting deep thoughts into simple words.

He received a thorough religious training in the Nazareth synagogue. He mastered the holy scriptures of his people and was early recognized locally as a religious personality and as a rabbi, or teacher.

At about the age of thirty, Jesus had an inner religious experience which brought to him an overwhelming awareness of the presence of God, and he felt impelled to proclaim that great reality far and wide to all people.

He then left Nazareth to set out on this high venture. He first visited a strange ascetic, John the Baptist, who lived on the banks of the river Jordan and sounded a call for repentance because "the Kingdom of God is at hand." Jesus responded with the request for immersion in the Jordan as a symbol of his own dedication to God.

The Gospels tell next the story of his withdrawal into the wilderness beyond the river Jordan to reflect on the path he must follow from there on. For forty days he wandered in the wilderness and fasted; and in thinking it through, he was sorely tempted. He rejected all three temptations: bread and security, power and glory, and dramatic means to win converts. He then returned to his home ground in the northern province of Galilee to begin his ministry. He preached and he taught. He healed, often so wondrously that he soon became famous for his miracles; and, always, he presented to people everywhere a most remarkable example of direct and practical kindness.

Jesus walked the common roads and talked in market places and synagogues, in wheat fields and on hill slopes. Thousands came to hear him and seek his help. The people drawn to him were moved by his bearing and outlook, as much as by what he said.

His key theme was the nearness of the Kingdom of God. By this most of his hearers took him to mean a sudden miraculous transformation of the earth and its inhabitants, to be expected in the near future when men would be judged for their thoughts and their acts. He spoke of a loving and forgiving God who was the Father of all mankind, both the source and the ruler of the universe. Complete faith in God meant inner security that would banish anxiety. God was in nature and in history, but also in a man's heart. Access to God came through penitence and prayer; penitence would engage the Father's forgiveness, while the prayers would lead to what Paul the Apostle was later to describe as "the peace which passeth all understanding."

Such thoughts were in accord with the centuries-old tradition in the Hebrew faith. This latter-day prophet, however, gave it new force. The Kingdom of God of which he spoke was accessible not only to his fellow Jews but to all mankind.

Christians consider Jesus to have been the long-promised Christ, The Anointed One, the Son of the Living God. It is certain that he himself was convinced that his was a unique mission, for he told the congregation of his boyhood

synagogue in Nazareth as he read Isaiah's words aloud from
the sacred scrolls:

". . . The Spirit of the Lord is upon me, because He
hath anointed me to preach the gospel to the poor; He
hath sent me to heal the brokenhearted, to preach de-
liverance to the captives, and recovering of sight to the
blind, to set at liberty them that are bruised, to preach
the acceptable year of the Lord."

With calm assurance he concluded, "This day is this
scripture fulfilled in your ears."

The content of Jesus' preaching, a love for one's fellow
man so all-forgiving and all-inclusive that it reflected God's
love for man, was as penetrating as the method of his teaching was effective. His method shone through in the instance
of his rebuking the crowd about to stone the woman "taken
in adultery, in the very act": "He that is without sin among
you, let him first cast a stone at her." And when the men
who "heard it, being convicted by their own conscience,
went out one by one, beginning at the eldest, even unto the
last," Jesus could say to the woman, "Neither do I condemn
thee: go and sin no more." It was also to be seen in the
prayer he uttered as the Roman soldiers crucified him:
"Father, forgive them, for they know not what they do."

He taught his precepts in words spoken privately to the
band of a dozen chosen intimates who walked with him
from town to town and in sermons to the thousands who
gathered to hear him declare such truths as the Beatitudes:
"Blessed are the pure in heart: for they shall see God. Blessed
are the peacemakers: for they shall be called the children of
God. Blessed are the meek: for they shall inherit the earth.
Blessed are they that mourn: for they shall be com-
forted. . . ."

No less powerful as a means of teaching were his picturesque stories which, in brevity and beauty, are without parallel in other faiths: the parables of the Good Samaritan, the Lost Coin, the Talents, and many other simple narratives. "Without a parable spake he not unto them."

Such methods and thoughts ran counter to some time-hardened views and practices of the Sadducees and the Pharisees and the lesser conflicting groups within Jewry. They offended and antagonized some of Jesus' inner following, notably Judas Iscariot. Judas entered at length into negotiations to betray the whereabouts of Jesus on a given day to powerful leaders among his enemies.

When Jesus turned toward Jerusalem at the time of the Passover feast, he warned his disciples that death awaited him. They, in turn, tried to dissuade him from his decision to return to the city but to no avail.

As he entered the great city, his popularity reached its zenith. The day was to be commemorated from that time on as Palm Sunday, for the Jewish multitudes are said to have "cut down branches off the trees and strewed them in the way, crying out, Hosanna in the highest."

The simmering revolt against Jesus started to come to the surface as he went into the temple "and began to cast out them that sold and bought in the Temple, and overthrew the tables of the moneychangers, and the seats of them that sold doves, and would not suffer that any man should carry any vessels through the Temple. And he taught, saying unto them, Is it not written, My house shall be called of all nations the house of prayer? But ye have made it a den of thieves."

On a Thursday evening, now observed as "Maundy Thursday," when Jesus celebrated the Passover feast with his disciples in an upper room on Mount Zion, he instituted the rite which has come to be known as the Lord's Supper or the Holy Communion. The story, which has been retold across all the centuries, has touching notes of resignation and faith, of bowing before the inevitability of his tragic destiny while yet trusting in the Eternal.

"And as they did eat, Jesus took bread, and blessed, and brake it, and gave to them, and said, Take, eat; this is my body.

"And he took the cup, and when he had given thanks, he gave it to them: and they all drank of it. And he said unto them, This is my blood of the new testament, which is shed for many. Verily I say unto you, I will drink no more of the fruit of the vine, until that day that I drink it new in the kingdom of God.

"And when they had sung a hymn, they went out into the Mount of Olives."

Judas, who had earlier left the company in the upper room, then achieved the betrayal he had planned. He came to the Garden of Gethsemane and pointed out Jesus to the police sent to apprehend him. Jesus was then taken before an impromptu court drawn from the Sanhedrin, the seventy-one men who composed the highest tribunal for religious and civil decisions among the Jewish people, and there he was sentenced to death for blasphemy. But Jewish courts were not permitted to carry out death sentences. Hence the case was referred to the Roman procurator, Pontius Pilate. Reluctant to enforce a sentence, on such dubious grounds, Pilate sent Jesus on to Herod Antipas, governor of Galilee, who happened to be in town at the time. Herod refused jurisdiction, however, and returned Jesus to Pilate.

Pilate is said to have announced, "I find in him no fault at all," and to have recommended Jesus' release, for the custom was to free a prisoner at the Passover season. The mob refused Pilate's offer and asked for the release of the robber Barabbas instead.

Diffidently and doubtfully, it appears, Pilate then remanded Jesus to the guards for crucifixion. Some hours later—in midafternoon—he died, having uttered the plaint, "My God, my God, why hast Thou forsaken me?" and the sigh of resignation, "It is finished."

One of his upper-class followers, Joseph of Arimathea, secured permission from Pilate to remove the body. With Nicodemus, another friend, he embalmed it and laid it in a sepulcher which Joseph had originally built to be his own tomb.

On Sunday, the third day of Jesus' death, some of his friends, scattered and forlorn, slowly straggled back and discovered the tomb to be empty. Suddenly, as they reported later, they saw an angel who told them Jesus had risen from his grave. Then, according to Simon Peter, Jesus appeared before him in person. Soon the news spread, and word went around that Jesus had risen from the dead. He had promised he would come again, and this promise was now fulfilled. Thus began this new faith, which brought to its devotees, as one of its most eloquent spokesmen wrote in later years to friends in Corinth, ". . . faith, hope, and love, these three; but the greatest of these is love."

The writer of these words was Paul or Saul of Tarsus, a tentmaker and something of a rabbinical scholar, who started the spread of the new religion on out into the non-Jewish Mediterranean world. Paul had not always been a devout follower of Christ. As an ardent Pharisee with all the reverence for Jewish Law this status entailed, he had witnessed and approved of the stoning to death of Stephen, the first great Christian martyr, and with the permission of the high priest in Jerusalem he had pursued to Damascus the followers of Christ. On that journey, as told in the Book of Acts in the New Testament, he experienced the conversion he never tired of telling about in his later ministry as the first Christian missionary. He had been struck blind, felled to the ground, and suffused with a blinding light. Then he heard the voice of Jesus: "Saul, Saul, why persecutest thou me?"

From that time on Saul's—or Paul's—life was completely altered and he soon became a leader among the followers of the risen Christ. The persecuter of the new religion had now become its foremost advocate to the world. He is often described as a "second founder of Christianity," because in the following thirty years he went on missionary journeys throughout the Mediterranean area, where he made many converts in all social classes. In important centers he organized communities of faith, or "churches," as congregations of Christians came to be called. He preached of the centrality of "Christ Jesus," whose presence within a man's heart would give a righteousness beyond any that could come merely through obedience to the Law and observance of it. Now, he believed, there was no longer any need to feel obliged by ritual regulations, for by Jesus' dying on the cross, a vicarious atonement, the Law had been fulfilled through love.

Inevitably he came into conflict with those disciples of Jesus who still relied upon the Jewish Law and, holding Jesus to be the long-awaited messiah, expected him to return again soon. Eventually his brand of Christianity became the more powerful and is known to us as the Pauline wing.

In his powerful, at times poetic, and always fervent letters to his churches, Paul outlined his new faith with a passion and a directness few Christians have been able to match in the centuries since. Despite the disparity of interpretations given to Paul's ideas, they were the major source of Christian thought. Doctrines were hammered out later but Paul was the first to undertake the interpretation of the Christian faith for the new world. Roman Catholic theology traces its norm to him, and Protestants also consider Paul the fount of their thought. Indeed, his major contribution was the welding together of the many divergent elements of the Christian movement in its earliest years:

". . . There is neither Jew nor Greek, there is neither bond nor free, there is neither male nor female; for ye are all one in Christ Jesus. . . . I, therefore, the prisoner of the Lord, beseech you that ye walk worthy of the vocation wherewith ye are called, with all lowliness and meekness, with long-suffering, forbearing one another in love; endeavoring to keep the unity of the Spirit in the bond of peace. There is one body, and one Spirit, even as ye are called in one hope of your calling; one Lord, one faith, one baptism, one God and Father of all, who is above all, and through all, and in you all."

Other interpreters of Christianity went elsewhere, moving west into the Greco-Roman world, northeast into the regions around the Tigris and Euphrates rivers, and southward to Ethiopia, though none surpassed Paul.

Governors in the provinces of the Roman Empire began to find this religion a vexation. Especially repellent to them was the Christians' refusal to join in emperor worship.

Persecution of Christians had taken place even as early as A.D. 64, when Nero had subjected them to public execution. It had become a common thing for the Roman government, especially in Asia Minor and the Levant, to burn

Christians at the stake or cast them to the lions. By A.D. 250 the Emperor Decius was imposing ruthless measures to exterminate Christianity. Intensified by the Emperor Valerian, the persecution mounted to its cruelest height under Diocletian at the beginning of the fourth century.

But within two decades the entire picture changed. When Constantine became the uncontested emperor of the realm in A.D. 323, Christians had already been granted by him —and by other aspirants for imperial authority—freedom of conscience and equality with all other religions. Constantine now restored properties to the Church, erected new churches, and so strongly supported the faith that, near the end of the fourth century, his successors recognized Christianity as the official religion of the empire.

Earlier (by the latter half of the second century) the Christian church had begun to be called "Catholic," thus signifying a "universal" church. The church did include men and women from all social classes, even in remote corners of the Roman territory; and it was to extend this inclusive reach into even more distant lands during the next thousand years. The Catholic Church modeled its administration on the system which secured the unity of the far-flung Roman Empire, and it built an ecclesiastical structure that ultimately proved to be stronger and more lasting even than empire because it possessed something more—a conviction of its uniqueness as a faith and its vocation to serve a world in which the power of the Roman secular government was crumbling.

The Catholic Church proceeded gradually to formulate its official doctrine in a theology which was declared to be not only logical but also without error. Anyone who deviated from this prescribed set of beliefs was denounced as a heretic; heresy was defined as any doctrine counter to

the dogmas of the Church. The unorthodox were condemned because they created schisms—that is, splits in the
unity of the faith. For centuries to come, the "true believers" hounded heretics, often to death.

The Emperor Constantine, intent on unifying both the
faith and the faithful within the Christendom which he
had legalized, convened the Council of Nicaea in A.D. 325.
This memorable assemblage of Christian leaders from the
Mediterranean region and Empire outposts adopted the
Nicene Creed, establishing for their contemporaries and for
posterity the dogma (that is, the official doctrine) that Jesus
Christ was the Savior, "begotten, not made, of the same
substance with the Father." This affirmation established the
trinitarian basis of orthodox Christianity: the godhead of
the Father, Son, and Holy Ghost was one in substance, or
essence, but functioning through three distinct though in-
terpenetrating persons. From that time on, the Church of
the West felt sure of itself. Its basic formula had been declared, and its adherents could continue their program of
conversion without quarrels or distractions.

The Eastern part of the Church was not satisfied with
these statements and adopted a slightly different formula.
The Council of Chalcedon of Asia Minor in A.D. 451 restated the issue concerning the divinity and humanity of
Christ and appeared to resolve the disagreements; but the
results led to the formation of various sects, notably the
Nestorians in India and Iran, the Coptic churches of Ethiopia and Egypt, the Melchites and Maronites of Syria and
present-day Lebanon, and the Jacobites of Iraq, Syria, and
India.

In the following centuries, until the Protestant Reformation, the Western or Roman Catholic Church constituted
by far the largest part of Christendom and manifested its

power by asserting authority through the papacy—that is, through the Bishop of Rome as its supreme head. Another source of strength for the Church in those post-Nicene centuries was the growth of monasticism—orders of men or of women who, in a manner reminiscent of the Essenes of Jesus' time, took vows of devotion to a communal life of worship and work, obedience to their superiors, and sexual abstinence. The products were the preservation of learning, a disciplined worship, informed meditation, and directed social service.

Parallel to the Popes' influence during the late fourth and early fifth centuries was that of an eminent intellectual, Augustine, Bishop of Hippo in North Africa. Once a luminary of the pagan world, Augustine was baptized on Easter of the year 387 by his mentor, the famed Ambrose of Milan. His explanations of the Trinity, his sense of the immediate presence of God, his conviction that Christ dwelt within him, and his belief in original sin were accepted by Catholic theologians and, retroactively, by most Protestant theologians also, after the Reformation. His outstanding work, *The City of God,* was written to defend Christianity against the charge that it was responsible for the successive setbacks the Roman Empire had experienced under the impact of mass invasions by barbarians from the north. In this vast book he drew a sharp distinction between such earthly cities as Babylon and Rome on the one hand and, on the other hand, the City of God, serving as a standard of judgment and an ideal.

In similar fashion, eight centuries later, Thomas Aquinas created the two foremost theological books of his era, the *Summa Contra Gentiles* and the *Summa Theologiae.* These unique achievements of the thirteenth century reconciled once for all, so Aquinas thought, the contrasts of Christ and

Aristotle, theology and philosophy, revelation and reason. Among the myriad propositions and counterpropositions, the most famous were Aquinas' five arguments to establish the existence of God. This elaborate edifice of thought did not, however, remain as conclusive and unassailable for future generations as Aquinas had hoped. Too many new forces were to erode his carefully articulated and systematized structure.

All the popes, monastic orders, and scholars of the later Middle Ages felt the effects of the Crusades, the series of wars undertaken by the Christians of Europe between the twelfth and fourteenth centuries to recover the Holy Land from the control of Islam. In 1095 at the Council of Clermont, Pope Urban II appealed to Christians to battle for the Holy Sepulcher and wrest it from the Moslems. The response was overwhelming: tens of thousands came from all over Western Europe, impelled in part by a misguided idealism but also by the desire for loot and booty. Many foresaw an expansion of territory for Western lands and the possibility of rich trade with peoples of the East. Not until 1291 did the "Latin kingdom of Jerusalem" fall; but this Crusaders' triumph of almost two centuries in duration only underscored the failure of the other Crusades.

Despite their pillaging and killing, the Crusades did leave a lasting impression on the Western world. Europe, the Occident, still far from sophisticated and somewhat uncivilized, learned much more about the Orient, and about Moslem Spain and the Near and Middle East, with their more luxurious living standards, wider trade, and not inconsiderable science. Unconsciously, perhaps even unintentionally, the Crusaders built a bridge between the Orient and the Occident.

In the Near and Middle East the Crusaders constructed

gigantic castles, many of which still stand, architecturally magnificent and structurally sound. They brought French to the Levant as the major language, a cultural heritage for which the Lebanese are grateful today. The Pope found his prestige enhanced and his position assured as the chief figure in a united Christian enterprise and in a unified Christendom. The Crusades influenced literature and art, giving the ideal of chivalry to poetry and prose, music and drama. Unfortunately they left a scar on the memory of the Moslem peoples which still makes them resentful of Christians, and they had a disastrous effect on the limited civil rights of Jews living in the midst of Christian Europe.

The Crusades and the fall of Constantinople in 1453 started an exodus of scholars to Italy; they took with them the masterpieces of the Greek world intact in the original Greek. This gave a powerful impetus to the movement, already under way for two centuries, which produced the Renaissance with its revival of classical learning. The humanism of the Renaissance, reflected in sculpture and painting, ballads and poetry, rejoiced in nature and in man.

The world had now grown apace; and the Church, in both its power and its claims to allegiance, faced a sharp challenge. No longer was it in a position to prescribe the requirements of the religious life, nor did it have an unquestioned monopoly of learning or knowledge.

The seeds of the Protestant Reformation had long been sown and soon would break forth in revolt. As early as the end of the twelfth and the beginning of the thirteenth centuries, dissent and discontent were apparent in the Waldensians and the Albigensians in northern Italy and southern France. The latter were named after the town of Albi, center of their efforts to return to purer religion, and the former named for the founder of the movement, Peter

Waldo, a merchant turned priest, who started a trend toward reform in organized religion.

Almost two centuries later the call for reform was heard in England from John Wycliffe. He denounced taxation by the popes and questioned the power or the right of a priest to alter the wine and the bread of the communion service as to make them the blood and the body of Christ; he translated the Bible into the English language, so that the common people might hear at first hand and read with their own eyes the words which "brought down the mighty from their seats and exalted those of low degree."

In Bohemia (part of Czechoslovakia now) Jan Hus followed in Wycliffe's train. Hus incited the people to rebel against the authority of the Church. In 1415 he was burned at the stake by order of the Council of Constance.

A great many other men sounded the cry for reform, but Martin Luther of Germany and John Calvin of France, later of Switzerland, remained as the two chief figures of the movement which split Christendom in two. Each would have denied any accusation that he had created a fissure but would have stoutly maintained that he sought to restore to the Church the purity and the integrity which he contended the Roman Catholics had already destroyed.

The Reformation spread then to France and the Netherlands, to Scotland and to England and brought about profound changes in each of these lands as opposing points of view, Roman Catholic versus Protestant, cast them into turmoil. The most vexing problem on both sides was to fulfill the time-honored imperative: ". . . rightly to divide the word of truth."

In similar fashion the Protestant radicals, composed of Anabaptists on the one hand and Unitarians on another, nonconformists in one direction and Puritans, Congregationalists, Baptists, and Quakers in still other directions, all reflected something of the yearning for freedom in the faith of Protestantism. Before the Pilgrims set out from Leyden on the *Mayflower* to sail the Atlantic to the New World in 1620, their spiritual leader, John Robinson, had predicted: "God hath yet more truth to emerge from his Holy Word." Each of the new sects, or "denominations," attested to the creative power which bursts forth from a religion grounded upon a personal allegiance—in this case to Jesus Christ—and no longer restrained by either pontiffs or kings.

There were dangers in such absence of external authority; for many the blessing of freedom soon became a bane. The age-old battle between freedom and order was repeatedly and painfully re-enacted.

By the middle of the sixteenth century, so many adherents and so much territory had been surrendered to the Protestants that Pope Paul III called together the Council of Trent in 1545. In the following eighteen years that famous gathering modified many Roman Catholic teachings, reaffirmed others, remedied some of the worst abuses of former centuries, and laid plans for a Catholic Reformation, in turn, in both thought and action. This Counter Reformation resulted in new directions and new movements within the Roman Catholic Church. One of the most important groups to emerge was the Jesuits under the leadership of the Spanish nobleman, Ignatius Loyola, whose soldier-like discipline (the "spiritual exercises") introduced sterner standards for the priesthood, along with an incomparable missionary zeal.

While Protestantism was assuming new forms during the eighteenth and nineteenth centuries, Roman Catholicism continued its own renewal and reformation, especially in the

ecumenical gathering convened in 1869–1870 and called
"Vatican Council I" (although, in fact, the twentieth in
the fifteen and a half centuries since the first council at
Nicaea). The most important developments for Roman
Catholics in the nineteenth century were the promulgation
by Pope Pius IX of a long-discussed doctrine, the Immac-
ulate Conception of the Virgin, and his pronouncement of
it as a dogma of the Church; and, some years later, in 1870,
his proclamation of the doctrine of Papal Infallibility.

Vast and far-reaching changes are occurring within the
Catholic Church during the second half of the twentieth
century. One noteworthy by-product of these changes is a
more friendly attitude toward the "separated brethren," the
Protestants. Great strides have been taken, too, in relating
the Christian faith to the findings of modern science and
in adapting the teachings of the Church to the hypothesis
of evolution. Pope Paul VI may appear to have begun to
brake the movement launched by Pope John XXIII in his
"updating" of the Church from 1958 to 1963 as he restrains
groups, ranging from the Jesuits to the "radicals," in their
zeal to modernize the thought and programs of the Church;
but it is more accurate to say that Pope Paul VI is in the
middle of an intense struggle within the Church between
conservative and liberal forces. On Protestantism in turn,
influences of modern science and the effects of industrialization have been enormous during the past two and a half
centuries.

The nineteenth century has been called "the great Protestant century" due to the outreach of Protestantism
through the missionary movement. Protestant foreign mis-
sions arose in the eighteenth century with the opening of
charted sea routes, following the example of the remarkably
successful Roman Catholic missionary priests in India,

China, and Japan in the sixteenth century. Both Protestants and Roman Catholics sent out representatives who had a deeply engaged devotion to the central Christian conviction that their most precious possession—God in Christ—should be shared with all who could be reached. The missionary enterprise became a worldwide program of Protestant churches. Coupled with missionary zeal was the movement to establish Sunday schools, encourage religious education among lay people, support the settlement house movement, and engage in social action to bring the judgments of religion to bear on the problems of the world: poverty, war, disease, illiteracy, and injustice.

Such developments in the last three centuries have left an indelible mark on all segments of Christianity: not only on the Roman Catholic and the historic Protestant sectors, but also on all branches of the Eastern or Orthodox Church and on the many Protestant sects of more recent origin. The "ecumenical" or World Church movement within Protestant circles has already resulted in bringing together many kindred denominations, and also in building tentative bridges between Catholics and Protestants. The latter overtures, long delayed and warmly welcomed, have been openly expressed by the attendance of authorized Roman Catholic observers at ecumenical gatherings of the Protestants' World Council of Churches in Evanston, Illinois, in 1954 and New Delhi, India, in 1961. At sessions of Vatican Council II in Rome, from 1962 to 1965, a large number of official Protestant "observers" were hospitably received and carefully briefed each day; these Protestants could be said to have had an informal but very real influence on the proceedings of the council.

A greater awareness of Christianity's debt to Judaism, its mother faith, has now begun to prevail among Christians, as

well as a sense of contrition for what Christians have done
(sins of commission) in persecuting the Jews, and have not
done (sins of omission) in failing to combat anti-Semitism
—most notably in remaining silent during the annihilation
of such a large percentage of European Jewry during the
Hitler period. Here is an entirely new dimension in Christian thinking and Christian doing. The ecumenical movement may be churchly in origin and emphasis, but it has
come to mean something that reaches far beyond the church,
namely an effort to achieve interfaith and inter-ethnic amity.

Like many another religion, Christianity has manifested
an extraordinary capacity to renew itself, to emerge from
ashes like the proverbial phoenix. The twentieth century
seems to be a time when Christianity as a whole is under-
going unprecedented changes. These mutations have proceeded so swiftly and so widely that many a Christian formerly dismayed by the passivity of the organized church,
baffled by the multiplicity of sects within Christianity, disillusioned by its seeming irrelevance, now marvels at these
swift currents of fresh vitality.

Christians hear anew an ancient phrase, reported in the
Book of Revelation as having come from the God whom a
simple country carpenter served: "Behold, I make all things
new!"

VIII
ISLAM

And Mohammed
Is His Prophet

ISLAM, preceded by two other religions of monotheism, Judaism and Christianity, originated in the seventh century A.D. and is therefore youngest among the universal religions of mankind. Its chief spokesman and interpreter was Mohammed, known as the Prophet, or one who "speaks for God." He chose the name Islam because in the Arabic language it implied "submission to or achieving peace with God," a major motif in the new faith he taught and followed.

Mohammed, one of the most dramatic figures in history, was born, according to tradition, in A.D. 570 in Mecca, in the Arabian Peninsula (now Saudi Arabia). Orphaned six years after his birth, he was raised by his grandfather, 'Abd-al-Muttalib, and his uncle, Abu Talib. Both men were leaders of the Quraysh tribe, trustees of the religious sites in Mecca, which was already a holy city because of the huge Black Stone, the cube-shaped shrine of Kaaba built around this meteorite, an abundance of idols, and the Sacred Well of Zamzam.

Aroused by the religious fervor of the region, Mohammed was at the same time detached from its intense excitement and frenetic observances. He became even more removed from these ancient customs and rites and critical of them when be began to travel along the Red Sea area and to learn about other religions. During his youth and young manhood he accompanied caravans from Southern Arabia to the borders of Jordan. The travels were of real significance for him, in part because he seems to have encountered Jewish scholars and Christian monks whom he heard expound their faiths before crowds at fairs, and partly because, at the age of twenty-four, he became the business manager of a wealthy widow named Khadijah, whom he married some years later.

Khadijah helped him through many of his religious conflicts, and in the atmosphere of leisure and comfort her wealth provided, he was encouraged to meditate and then to write about his thoughts and visions. During Khadijah's lifetime Mohammed, who sanctioned polygamy, did not allow himself any other wife; only after her death did he marry again, including among his several wives a Jewish girl, a Coptic Christian, and the former wife of an adopted son.

At the age of forty, he began to be seized by the conviction that he had been chosen by God to be the prophet of true religion among the Arabs. The Arabs, unlike other peoples, had known no prophet before him, but now he was the choice. For days Mohammed remained alone in a cave on Mount Hira, a short distance north of the city of

Mecca. Suddenly, his later recollections recorded, the arch-angel Gabriel came to him in a vision as a messenger of God and told him to preach. Variously translated as "cry out" or "recite" or "read," the words "speak out" came to Mo-hammed's consciousness: *Speak out in the name of the Lord who created. . . . Speak out . . . for the Lord is the most Beneficent and has taught the use of the pen.*

Here began the Koran (meaning "The Word") or Qur'an, a spelling which resembles more closely the correct pronunciation. From that time on, Mohammed's revelations were recorded and then collected in this sacred book of the Moslems, their version of the Word of God which to any reader, no matter what his faith, has a haunting charm, a lyric beauty and rhythmic flow of almost hypnotic power.

Though reassured by his devoted Khadijah and by her cousin, a blind old man, who was quite possibly a Christian, Mohammed went through months of anguish and self-doubt; but recurrences of his visions and revelations con-vinced him that he was indeed "the Prophet of Allah, the One and Only God." The utterances Allah impelled him to reveal were, he believed, even more important than those given to Jews and Christians, for they were meant primarily for Arabians.

In Mecca, center of the Quraysh tribe and site of the Kaaba idol worship, his hearers were not impressed. They resented his preachments against the 354 idols (one for every day of their lunar year) and his inveighing against the superstitious practices of the time. To their resentment they added resistance; about A.D. 620 his plight was at its worst. Moreover, his wife Khadijah had died; and shortly there-after occurred the death of his uncle Abu Talib, a strong and loyal ally.

Yet within two years Mohammed's fortunes began to

improve. He found friends and supporters in nearby Medina, the prosperous oasis then still known as Yathrib. These
allies made him their newly chosen overlord; in A.D. 622,
he swiftly migrated there from Mecca in the famous flight
known thereafter as the Hegira (the migration). Mohammed built the first mosque in that city and established the
customs of holding a weekly "Sabbath" service on Friday,
facing Mecca for prayer, and giving alms to the poor.

Now Yathrib officially became Medina—that is, *Ma-
dinat an nabi,* "the City of the Prophet"—and it served as
the base for Mohammed's campaign against Mecca. When,
in January of 630, he conquered Mecca, Mohammed had
become the foremost man in Arabia.

Two years later—in 632—Mohammed was dead; by
that time, however, his power had been firmly established.
He had united the tribes of Arabia under a regime which
acknowledged the Will of Allah as the one and only God,
and he had established the brotherhood of all Moslems. For
two years all Arabia was in revolt, but by A.D. 634 his op-
ponents were gone; for all had been put to the sword. Reluctant converts, recalcitrant and refractory, were better
dead, especially the two aspiring prophets, Tallah and Mu-
saylimah. Mohammed's closest companion and disciple,
Abu Bakr, became the Caliph—"successor"—as political
and religious leader of Islam. During the two years of rule
before his death Abu Bakr led the crusade as Islam moved
swiftly to secure more converts and conquer additional
territory.

First in his lifetime and then after his death by the power
of his followers, Mohammed had united the Bedouins, no-
madic desert tribes in Arabia. They were now welded into a
lightning-like, invincible military unit which moved out of
the desert into the more prosperous lands of the Middle

East. Opposing tribal chieftains either came to terms with Mohammed's followers or perished as the Moslem armies moved out into the Levant, conquered Damascus in A.D. 635, and then, a century later, took over Spain.

In the following centuries there developed an intellectual ferment which was to have far-reaching effect: the great philosophical achievement of Islam. The Arabian Avicenna (980–1037) and the Spanish-Arabian Averroës (1126–1198) and other Moslem scholars helped to perpetuate Greek thought in Europe and preserve the works of such philosophers as Plato and Aristotle. Without this Islamic contribution the thinkers of the Middle Ages would have been deprived of the writings of the Greeks, and the thought of such great men as the Jew Maimonides and the Christian Aquinas would have been without substance and meaning. Aided by a number of Jewish scholars, Moslem intellectuals translated the Greek works into Syriac, Aramaic, or Hebrew, and then rendered them into Arabic; in some instances both the Greek and the Arabic versions are no longer extant and only the Hebrew renditions are available. The Western world is deeply indebted to those Moslem intellectuals and philosophers for this legacy.

By the eighth century the center of the Moslem world lay in Baghdad of Iraq. Under the leadership of the famed Caliph Harun-al-Rashid, this "abode of peace" at the "crossroads of the world," became known in both East and West as one of the greatest of cities. A commercial center and a scholars' abode, Baghdad experienced varying fortunes; despite a steady decline it remained the strong core of Islam until the Mongolian invasion in the mid-thirteenth century. Then the Arab-dominated Moslem world lost both power and unity, giving way to the Ottoman Turks, the Persians, and the Mogul emperors of India.

The Ottoman Empire gradually took possession of the area, captured Constantinople, and controlled the strategic Bosphorus. Under the impulse of Islam the Turks invaded Europe as far as the city of Vienna where, in the decisive battle of 1683, they were defeated. Had the Turks won, all of Europe would doubtless have become Moslem. The Turks then withdrew into their Middle Eastern empire which remained comparatively intact until World War I. In 1917–1918 the Allies, mostly under British leadership, destroyed its power and divided the Middle East into smaller states destined in the following years to become independent according to "self-determination" under the aegis of mandates granted by the League of Nations. Turkey itself became a completely secular state in the 1920s; and Islam, long the dominant influence, assumed a minimal status.

The power of Islam was not stayed by the rise of the secular government in Turkey or by the decline of its authority in such lands as Egypt, for today an estimated 450,-000,000 people accept its tenets. In the continent of Africa its numbers grow apace, at least ten times as swiftly as Christianity's, for Islam knows no distinctions of race and attracts black men, inclined to be repelled by Christianity. Islam seems more authentic to many Africans and is more closely linked to African social life, especially with its polygamy, than is the more austere, monogamous Christian way of life. Yet Blacks in Africa are discovering that the Moslem faith has not restrained Arabs from exploiting and even enslaving them.

Islam is a leading religion in much of Asia, including not only the Moslem states of Pakistan and Malaya, but also parts of Indonesia, the Philippines, Iran, Afghanistan, and Iraq, all of the Arab states, and portions of the Soviet Union and India. Quite apart from its large numbers of followers in Asia, the Middle and Near East, and Africa, Islam has a sizable foothold in such European areas as Turkey and Albania, parts of the Crimea and the former state of Bosnia, now part of Yugoslavia.

What was and is this faith which blazed with such fire, spread with such speed, conquered with remarkable success, and still elicits a loyalty of such fervor and fidelity? In contrast to the diverse, often bizarre religious practices of the Arabian world into which Mohammed was born 1400 years ago, it was an explicit, forthright set of beliefs and practices which emerged in the first decade of this new religion. With singularly little change, these beliefs have remained constant in the subsequent thirteen and one-third centuries.

Mohammed's teachings were the basic foundation for his followers' beliefs. Explained with simplicity, though not always with clarity, they were outlined in the Koran. In accordance with the meaning of Islam—namely, the way of submission—the Moslem was expected to believe without question or argument. By so doing he guaranteed his salvation in this world and in the next.

God the Creator and Judge came first, last, and always. He was all-powerful and all-knowing, all-merciful and all-compassionate. He was—and is—supreme. He is One.

The Moslem differs from the Christian in his concept of God because trinitarian formulas of "God the Father, God the Son, and God the Holy Ghost" are, in the Moslem's view, polytheistic. A Moslem calls God "Father," and thinks of him as "love," attributes which overshadow those of might and majesty. Allah, say the prayers of Moslems and the verses of the Koran, is both the Lord of the Day of Judgment and the maker of the universe, the ruler of the world and the lord of all life. A Moslem will repeat the ninety-nine beautiful names of God and, when asked if there is a one hundredth, answers, "Only the camel knows it and that secret gives the camel his dignity." When a Moslem counts the beads of his prayer necklace, he tells them one by one on three sets of 33 each; he construes the total of 99 to comprise the human lexicon of names for the Almighty. In its uncompromising monotheism, with its simple enthusiastic love of God and submission to his will, Islam finds its strength.

Moslems believe in angels. Through them Allah reveals his will, as in the instance of the leading angel, Gabriel, who, as an emissary of God's revelations, brought the Koran to Mohammed. Similarly Azrael is the Angel of Death, and Asrafel will blow the trumpet when the Judgment Day is at hand. Allah, as portrayed by Mohammed, occupies a throne of eminence in the seventh heaven; He has about Him a host of angels who wait upon Him and do His bidding. Among these are Nakir and Munkar, entrusted with the task of subjecting every dead person in his grave to an examination. Preparations for these tests have been made by the recording angels, two of whom are assigned to each person and charged with listing deeds, both good and evil. All the angels, born of light, are capable of reason and decision.

Satan, a variation on *Shaytan* of the Zoroastrians and also known as *Iblis* (in contracted form from the word *Diabolos*), became the Devil when evicted from the Garden of Eden; he had failed to obey God's command to show respect to Adam, a fallen angel. His task is to tempt men and to impede the purposes of Allah. The Devil is doomed to failure, however, for not only does Allah know all, but He wills

everything, including the most nefarious machinations and
devious maneuvers of the Devil. Ultimately the victory be-
longs to Allah, not the Devil.

In this world of spirit and spirits there are *genii* or *jinn*
(*jinnis*). Often they are of good intentions; but for the most
part they are troublemakers and evildoers. As Mohammed
is the messenger of Allah and angels are the doers of His
will, so the Koran is His means of revelation. The Koran,
written in Arabic, is God's revelation to Mohammed; therefore it is the object of devotion for all Moslems everywhere.
It cancels and replaces all previous revelations, among which
Moslems number the respected but rejected Old and New
Testaments. Only the Koran is genuine and holy; it is Truth
absolute. Though derived in considerable part from both
Jewish and Christian sources, the Koran is to the Moslem
the unalloyed Word of Allah.

The Moslems believe that Allah has revealed himself in
a progressive succession through His prophets. Although
men may not heed such prophets, God forgives them and
continues to send new prophets of whom Mohammed is
the culmination, the final revelation. If mankind fails to
heed the revelation of Islam, the end of the world is soon at
hand. To lead up to this last judgment, God has sent six
great prophets, each of whom has a special relationship to
Allah: Adam, "The Father of Man"; Noah, "The
Preacher"; Abraham, "The Chosen"; Moses, "The Friend
of God"; Jesus, "The Spirit of God"; and Mohammed,
"The Apostle." Each of the six is thus related in specially
chosen titles to Allah; but Mohammed himself is given the
center of the stage and scores of honoring names describe
him: "Peace of the World"; "Seal of the Prophets";
"Glory of the Ages"; etc. Although 124,000 prophets
have come from Allah to the human race, Mohammed is

foremost. Not only did he exist before the world was created and not only was he without sin (despite his prayers that his own sins be forgiven); but he could perform all manner of miracles, some of which are in the Koran but others in the *Ahadith* or *Traditions*, a collection of legends and not wholly authenticated information concerning Mohammed's life and Islam's rise.

To the Moslem, Mohammed is not so much the Anointed One as the Messiah is in Christian tradition, but rather the Appointed One, chosen by Allah to wash away heresies, ban false teachings, and replace former revelations. Doctrines stemming from Adam and the prophets were now revived and purified, completed and perfected.

Central to a Moslem's faith is his belief that every occurrence in life, whether good or bad, has been determined long in advance by the immutable order of Allah. Many a Moslem thinker contends that Allah is the author of evil, too, and that man has no free will. Moslems therefore tend to face life with an innate fatalism; and when burdened by poverty, scourged by illness, oppressed by tyrannies, or hobbled by circumstance, they accept their "fate."

The submission concept in the Moslem's faith stems from his belief in the judgment day. Of this signal and awesome event Mohammed preached often, and on it he centered much of his teaching. Both in the Koran and in later writings of Islam, the last day, the day of reckoning, is the focal point. Moslems are warned that their wrongdoings will be balanced against good and meritorious deeds. Not unlike those of the Zoroastrians, the descriptive warnings of the last judgment tell of the soul's crossing a vast bridge which is as sharp as a sword, as thin as a hair, and as long as a caravan's journey. The evildoer is destined to fall into hell-fire beneath, but the good and righteous will quickly move into paradise. The Koran and subsequent Islamic writings describe in picturesque, persuasive detail the celestial gardens of the afterlife which will abound with succulent fruits, rivers of rare wine, and lovely women, all in stark contrast to the fiery torments of hell.

To avoid the fires of hell and be eligible for paradise, the Moslem accepts five religious duties, the Pillars of Islam, which are inescapable obligations: (1) repetition of his witness to Allah; (2) recital of specific prayers; (3) observance of Ramadan, the month of fasting; (4) distribution of alms; and (5) the pilgrimage to Mecca.

The good Moslem repeats the basic creed of Islam ("There is no god but Allah, and Mohammed is his prophet") all his life long, from infancy till death. The dying man seeks to utter these as his final words before expiring; and the bereaved whisper them into his ears after he has drawn his last breath. These eleven words, taken from two separate parts of the Koran, have elicited a single-mindedness and fanaticism unparalleled in any other religion. Although the believer recites them by rote several times daily and a hundred thousandfold more times during a long life, the true Moslem is expected to have at least one sublime occasion during his lifetime when he utters them with complete understanding and wholehearted acceptance.

Five times a day the Moslem prays—at the rising of the sun, at noonday, in the middle of the afternoon, as twilight merges into night, and after dark. No matter where he is, whether on desert sands or country road or city street, at work bench or study table, the Moslem washes his hands, face, and feet with water (if water is unavailable, then with sand), faces Mecca, spreads his prayer rug, removes his shoes and covers his head; then he begins the prayers according to a specified, traditional formula: first in a stand-

ing position he holds extended hands beside his head and
then crouches to a semiseated position on his haunches,
finally prostrating himself so that knees and toes are on the
floor or ground while his hands are spread and his head is
touching a prayer stone, made of baked earth from one of
the holy places of Islam and carried with him everywhere.

Although the five prayers to be said are different in various parts of the Islamic world, they are all repeated in response to the call for prayer cried out from the minaret by
a muezzin. Vast numbers of Moslems move to the mosque
on Friday noonday as though drawn by a magnet to hear
the stated prayers, ponder readings from the Koran, listen to
a sermon, and join in uttering the words of their most familiar prayer, the opening lines of the Koran:

> In the name of Allah, the merciful, the compassionate.
> Praise be to Allah, the Lord of the Worlds,
> The merciful, the compassionate, the ruler of the Judg-
>   ment Day!
> Thee we serve and Thee we ask for aid,
> Guide us in the right path,
> The path of those to whom Thou art gracious;
> Not of those with whom Thou art wroth;
> Nor of those who err.

Ramadan, the ninth month of the Moslem lunar year,
requires fasting during the daytime and permits food only
in the hours from dusk till dawn. The familiar method of
determining when the fast should begin is to discern at
dawn the difference between a white thread and a black
thread when held at arm's length; and to terminate the fast
at the end of the day one should no longer be able to dis-
tinguish the white thread from the black. A cannon is fired
to denote the end of the day and the beginning of drinking

and eating. There is no set date for Ramadan because the lunar year is shorter than the solar year, and its ninth month therefore occurs in different seasons through the years. The sick and physically weak, soldiers and some essential laborers are exempted from keeping the fast; but Ramadan is in any case not a strictly observed fasting time.

Mohammed not only encouraged gifts of alms to the poor but practiced almsgiving himself. His followers consider the giving of legal alms as meritorious and distribute them at the end of a journey, the birth of a child, a marriage within the family circle, the occurrence of good fortune, or the observance of a holiday. In countries where Islam is the state religion, the state collects offerings of cattle, grain, fruit, etc. The almsgiving, usually known as *Zakat* or *Zakah,* is for the most part a voluntary matter now; but social pressure, plus a man's conviction of its basic merit, is a potent force for continuance of the custom. Centuries ago, when Islam was young, the almsgiving to beggars and slaves, strangers and debtors, institutions and charities, was considered "a loan to Allah"; and the proceeds were assigned to various deserving individuals and institutions by the religious officials who had placed these gifts in a general purse. In our time these donations, still widely expected and still generously given, are, however, voluntary in nature.

The last Pillar of Islam, and one of the most prestigious, is the pilgrimage to Mecca expected of every Moslem who is financially and physically able to make the journey. At least once in his life he must take this *hajj* (pilgrimage)— but only during the first to twelfth days of the last month in the lunar year, when during the seventh to the tenth days ceremonies in Mecca are observed. Some privileged Moslems, such as the King of Saudi Arabia and his retinue of wives and concubines and relatives, visit Mecca each year, but most consider themselves blessed of Allah if they can make a single pilgrimage during a lifetime. In Mecca a pilgrim meets fellow Moslems from all over the world, re-affirming Mohammed's preachments about the brotherhood of believers in Allah. He practices the usual ablutions, puts on the required two seamless tunics, accepts neither food nor drink during the daytime, refrains from sexual relations, and promises not to harm any living thing. First he goes to the Great Mosque and in its court kisses the Black Stone of the Kaaba, the small stone structure containing this sacred meteorite which is alleged to have been given to Abraham by the angel Gabriel. With thousands of others he encircles the Kaaba seven times, three of which are rapid and four slow. He repeats the special prayers, visits the Place of Abraham, and then goes to the Sacred Well to drink the waters. He may now consider himself greatly blessed. Next comes the so-called Lesser Pilgrimage: seven times he runs between the hills of Safa and Marwa, recalling Hagar in search of water for her infant child Ishmael. Then he pays a visit to Arafat, embarking on the Greater Pilgrimage by foot and devoting hours to meditation on the open plain. By nightfall he has returned with the shouting, clamoring mul-titudes of pilgrims to Minah where he throws the traditional seven pebbles at three pillars of masonry, called the "First," the "Middle Pillar," and the "Great Devil." He offers the animal sacrifice on the feast day, shares it with rich and poor alike, and, with the other pilgrims, visits Mohammed's grave in Medina. After three days of feasting he comes back to Mecca and once again encircles the Kaaba. From now on he may carry a special title, *Haj;* for the rest of his days he is distinguished for having made the pilgrimage to Mecca.

Such a religion, simple and direct though it may be, has

always been in danger, because of its formal nature and rigid requirements, of jeopardizing its spiritual assets. To offset such dangers the Sufi movement arose, in part in the eighth century but most powerfully at the end of the eleventh and beginning of the twelfth centuries. Led by the great theologian of Persia, "the Saint Augustine of Islam," Abu-Hamid Mohammed al-Ghazzali, this mystical movement expressed in lyric fashion the union of the soul with God. The name Sufi derived from "wool-wearers," the name given to these men who wore robes made of rough coarse wool. Sufism was not merely literary in nature but also philosophical as well, for it emphasized both asceticism and quietism. Some Sufis were virtually atheists as they absorbed ideas and influences from Buddhism; a number, in fact, advocated self-destruction. Their beliefs in extreme forms were pantheistic and opposed a basic concept of Islam: a centered idea of one God. The Sufis were intent, however, on achieving union with God in this present life rather than in an afterlife. By the twelfth century the Sufis had their own monasticism, requiring celibacy and meditational discipline. They created rituals of their own, leaning more toward the influencing faiths of Hinduism, Buddhism, Neo-Platonism, and Christianity than toward Islam.

From the Sufis came the dervishes, who might be called the monks of Islam. Many different orders of dervishes sprang up, some of them resembling the friars of Christianity but lacking their vows and avoiding the organization of monasteries. Their mystical beliefs found expression in the practices of whirling and howling by dervishes who considered themselves to be special beneficiaries of the favor of Allah. One of the most gifted of the Persian poets of Islam was Jalal-ud-Din Rumi of the thirteenth century, a dervish who wrote of the ineffable oneness a mystic feels with God.

If Christendom is blighted by the multiplicity of its sects, then Islam bears the same curse. Yet there is an essential unity to Islam, underscored by the annual pilgrimages to Mecca. At its best Islam is divided in two between the Shi'ites and Sunnites. Behind their differences—and linking them with the Sufis—is, first of all, the Koran; then the Five Pillars of Islam, most notably the five-times-a-day prayers and the Mecca pilgrimage; and, lastly, the festivals in the Moslem year, such as the end of the feast of Ramadan, the Great Feast near the close of the pilgrimage to Mecca, the New Year's festival, the Prophet's birthday, and the Prophet's night journey.

The difference between Shi'ites and Sunnites exposes, however, a basic cleavage which occurred in Islam's first centuries in disputes about the caliphate in successsion to Mohammed. The Sunnites, usually described as being the more traditional, defend the *Sunna*—that is, the fundamentals of Islam. They consider the Sunna to be the example of the prophet Mohammed, consisting not only of many reported sayings of Mohammed but also of anecdotes about him, thus supplementing the Koran. Variations in reporting these traditions have caused bitter clashes among Moslems, but they have been resolved by the so-called "agreement of Islam," known as the *Ijma*. The three—the Koran, the Sunna, and the Ijma—are the foundation stones of Islam. From the beginning a nucleus, ultimately to be known as the Shi'ites, diverged from the norm to disagree with the Sunnites. Mohammed's cousin and son-in-law, 'Ali, was the crux of the disagreement. The more orthodox Sunnites reject the Shi'ites' assertions about Mohammed and 'Ali, especially in ascribing to 'Ali powers akin to Mohammed's. Bitter persecutions afflicted the Shi'ites; often the group went underground and resorted to violent resistance. Yet unity persists in Islam, and conflicts between Sunnites and Shi'ites pale into insignificance before the power and the prestige of a basically unified Islam.

Another group with a Moslem heritage and originating during the late fifteenth and early sixteenth centuries was the Sikhs. They looked to the Hindus too for their religious nurture. They may appear to the world as tall men of soldierly bearing and with impressive beards and turbans, but beneath this surface impression lie a colorful history and a profound conviction. They revere Kabir (1450–1518), the saintly poet and weaver-mystic of northern India, the Sikh who tried to follow an Islamic bent while contending that a man need not be ensnared by the law of karma. The love of God sufficed for a man's salvation:

"Go where you will, to Benares or to Madura. If you do not find God in your own soul, the world is meaningless for you."

A generation later came Nanak; unlike Kabir, of Hindu forebears, he taught that repeating the true name of God was sufficient. There was no need to adhere either to Hinduism or Islam:

"Religion consisteth not in a patched coat, or a Yogi's staff, or in ashes smeared over the body. . . . Abide pure amid the impurities of the world; thus shalt thou find the way of religion."

Moslems combated Sikhism with such vehemence that Sikhs now hate Islam and Mohammedans.

In the Middle East, two groups that have emerged from Islam are of special interest: the Druses and the Bahais. Both reflect the creativity, durability, and resilience of Islam.

In the nineteenth century the Druses sprang from the movement which had responded to Hakim abu-'Ali Mansur, the insane caliph of the Fatimids who considered himself an incarnation of God. When he vanished, apparently a victim of a murder plot, the Druses considered him to have departed in order to return later as a divinely appointed ruler. Centered for the most part in Syria and Israel, 100,-000 in the former and about 40,000 in the latter, they have secret rites which are Islamic in origin.

From Persia emerged the Bahai movement which is to be traced mostly to the Shi'ites, but is now cut off from Islam and considers itself wholly independent. More than a century ago, Mirza ali Mohammed named himself Bab-ud-Din, "Gate of the Faith," and gathered many followers who called themselves Babis after him. Like a John the Baptist, he called his work a preparation for one greater than himself. Executed in 1850 for his heretical statements—primarily that his own writings exceeded the Koran in beauty and authority and because he demanded vast reforms—he was replaced by one of his followers who adopted the name Baha'u'llah ("the glory of God"). Some years later Baha'u'llah proclaimed himself the religious figure of whom Bab-ud-Din had foretold. His followers, now known as Bahais, followed him into exile after his flight from Baghdad; and the Turks then put him in the Acre prison for life. From there, however, his writings went into many lands and exerted wide influence because of their aim of inclusiveness, a kind of liberal universalism, and the call to all religions to unite. Each religion, the Bahais maintain, has some truth, and all religious leaders witness to truth, especially to the brotherhood of men beneath One God. Today Bahais have a magnificent gold-domed temple and archives in their Persian gardens on the slopes of Mount Carmel in Haifa, Israel; and in Wilmette, Illinois, on the shore of Lake Michigan, they have built an impressive and lovely temple.

Islam as a whole undergoes vast changes in these times,

some of them reviving the faith, others reforming its practices. To many, Islam seems remote and detached, obsolete and irrelevant; but to millions of others, the basic tenets of Islam have been and are being restated in the light of the introduction of Western ideas and practices. Certainly Islam grows in numbers, perhaps even in influence.

At the heart of Islam is the tie to the Judaeo-Christian tradition. As Jews and Christians echo the familiar verse of the 111th Psalm, "The fear of the Lord is the beginning of wisdom," so Moslems repeat the lines from the Koran: "The head of wisdom is the fear of Allah."

CONCLUSION

We Are the Heirs

A S HUNDREDS of generations passed by, many religions came into being and grew to power. Sometimes they shrank into obscurity, then loomed large again on the stage of history. Through the centuries, as countless millions of men and women lived and died, none of them—kings and chieftains, rich men or poor—lasted so long in the memories of mankind or influenced minds and hearts so profoundly as did Mahavira, Gautama Buddha, Confucius, Lao Tse, Socrates and Plato and Aristotle, the Hebrew prophets and Jesus, Zoroaster and Mohammed. They led in the search for meaning, the quest for balance within and assurance without.

To the average person in the West, the religions of the East are life-denying, while religions of the West, especially

161

Judaism and Christianity, emerging from the Middle East, seem to be life-affirming. Religions of the East appear to offer an escape from the torment of life and the endless cycle of rebirth, while the religions of the West often tend to escape into a life hereafter. These are generalizations, but the religions of the East can be said to be for the most part introverted; those of the West, extroverted.

In some respects, religions of the West are parallel to religions of the East. Each is engaged in a search for salvation. Each seeks to develop ethical standards (although Hinduism considers this an objective of lesser importance, so much so that the great humanitarian Albert Schweitzer called it a non-ethical religion). Each desires to know what purpose and value life holds. Each wants some measure of reconciliation and comfort when death strikes.

The West lacks much which Eastern religions possess. The Westerner is not aware of what solace, even inspiration, comes to the Easterner in contemplating the transmigration of souls; nor is he fully appreciative of the spiritual heights and depths a man of the East knows in his immersion in mysticism. Men of the West are too activist and impatient to embark on the meditational disciplines the East has developed.

We of the West admire but do not adopt the open-mindedness about other faiths (whether of East or West) which is so widely prevalent in the Orient. The narrow-mindedness and exclusivism so characteristic of Western religions caused Mahatma Gandhi to write that, after long study and experience, he had come to the conclusion that all religions are true and that all religions have some error in them: "My veneration for other faiths is the same as for my own faith. Consequently, the thought of conversion is impossible. . . . Our prayer for others ought never to be: 'God! Give them the light Thou hast given to me!' but:

'Give them all the light and truth they need for their highest development!' ''

The affinity among religions is not apparent in creeds and ceremonies, but it is clearly reflected in the area of ethics—that is, on the level of man's relationship to his fellow man. Note the striking parallels among all faiths with their versions of the Golden Rule.

The Hindu reads in the *Mahabharata:* "This is the true rule of life and the sum of duty: do nothing unto others which might cause you pain if it were done to you. Guard and do by the things of others as they do by their own."

The Buddhist finds counsel in the *Udana-Varga:* "Do not hurt others in any way that you would find hurtful. Seek for others the happiness you desire for yourself."

Confucius, as reported in the *Analects,* asked: "Is there one word of counsel by which one should act throughout his whole life?" He then answered: "It is indeed loving-kindness; do not unto others what you would not have them do unto you."

The Taoists, the *T'ai Shang Kan Ying P'ien* relates, must consider their neighbor's gain as their own and their neighbor's loss as their own.

Judaism has cherished Hillel's response, recorded in the Talmud: "What is hateful to you, do not to your fellow-man. That is the entire Law; all the rest is Commentary."

The Zoroastrian follows the words of the *Dadistan-i-dinik:* "Only that nature can be considered good which refuses to do unto another what is not good for itself. Do as you would be done by."

The Christian recalls the words of Jesus in his Sermon on the Mount of the Gospel According to Matthew: "All things whatsoever ye would that men should do to you, do ye even so to them."

The Moslem knows from the *Sunna* that no man is a

believer until he desires for his brother that which he desires for himself: "Let none of you treat his brother in a way he himself would not like to be treated."

The inhabitants of Greece and the Hellenic world taught: "Do not that to a neighbor which you shall take ill from him."

The Stoic of ancient Rome held that "the law imprinted on the hearts of all men is to love the members of society as themselves."

Each of these ten renditions of the Golden Rule points to a concern for others, a consideration for another's needs. One of these faiths, Christianity, has suggested that to make the Golden Rule of real significance, one should "do unto others *more* than one expects from another"; that one should give of one's self in love and in service without expectation of reward. That noble goal is seldom achieved, however, for among Christians as among most people, no matter what their faith, self-interest is too often the rule rather than the exception.

In sharp distinction to these parallels of the Golden Rule are the startling, often harsh contrasts among religions that no sentimental appeals to brotherhood can resolve. Virtually every faith vies with every other for supremacy. Some religions lay claim to being the sole revelation of God and to being, therefore, superior to all other faiths.

Religion often becomes a divisive factor, leading to hatred and conflict instead of mutuality and harmony. The competition still prevailing among Protestant denominations is destructive and damaging, as disheartening as the clashes between Shi'ites and Sunnites in Islam; and within the seemingly unified structure of Roman Catholic Christianity, tensions and jealousies exist in dismaying fashion among the orders. As the Apostle Peter said to his fellow Christians of nineteen centuries ago, "The time has come for judgment to begin in the House of God!"

Within every vital religion, no matter how commonplace or novel, venturesome or prosaic, there lies the aspiration toward the suprahuman, toward the Divine. In the Far East such religions as Hinduism, Buddhism, Confucianism, and Taoism (despite the strong non-theistic views of certain elements) have defined the Highest as a force infinite in extent, quite impossible of exact description, but still accessible by intuition. When a religionist of the Far East thinks of the Divine, he relies more on an intuition of what constitutes divinity. He defines his deity as something sensed with immediacy, felt to be a part of one's being, immanent and thus all-pervading, all-encompassing but yet incapable of being determined or described with exactitude, even by means of rich imagery.

On the other hand, the three major religions from the Middle East—Judaism, Christianity, and Islam—have construed God to be a force equally infinite but related more directly, determined more rationally, and within the historical context interpreted more logically. They refer to God as a Reality more adequately portrayed in doctrines and ideas, more precisely, even poetically, defined in intellectual terms. They stand in awe and wonder but seek the Word in articulate form, in specific words. While in the Far East the emotional aspects of reverence for God find greatest, most fervent expression, it is in the Middle East that there is more emphasis on the intellect, on the use of rational resources to describe, and thus ultimately to revere, God.

The Sacred, the Holy, the Divine, the Numinous are only four of the words used by teachers and leaders of religion through the centuries to describe the workings of God. Man's awareness of that Force can make for single-minded devotion and complete absorption in a cause. It can inspire the individual to ascend to heroic heights of courage, give up life in the most sublime self-sacrifice, or sustain a ceaseless search for meaning.

Dangers lurk here, however, for in the pursuit of such ends there always lies the possibility of a distortion of values. History is full of examples of excesses committed in the name of religion: human sacrifice among the ancients, as well as among such recent peoples as the Aztecs; cruelty and vengeance in the Inquisition, whether Medieval or Spanish; witch hunts of bizarre sorts, often of monstrous proportions; abuse of power and privilege.

The established religions of our time have faced a challenge and a threat in the rise of what have been popularly called "quasi-religions." These substitute religions surged to new levels of strength in the late nineteenth century and in the first two thirds of the twentieth century. One striking example was—and is—nationalism, always a focal point of men's allegiance. For other individuals a devotion to science or democracy, humanity or art became a substitute for formal religion, an alternative to the traditional religions of previous centuries.

The belief in the all-sufficient efficacy of technology is one such "faith," and for many millions of people throughout the world the natural sciences are the sole answer to the age-old question, "What is truth?" To these devotees of technology, the physical sciences contain all there is to know of reality. Life and the universe are explained on that mechanical level. The abstract sciences and the concrete sciences (physical and biological) are for them both the source of explanation and the object of devotion.

Many men of these modern times, finding it impossible to believe in a God and preferring to place their belief solely in man and his highest attributes, look to the scientific method for their explanation of life; they consider this to be enough, an adequate means by which they can create for themselves satisfactory lives. There are tens of millions, perhaps even hundreds of millions, who consider Protagoras' dictum, "Man is the measure of all things," to be sufficient explanation of their faith. To them the beliefs and practices of the religions surveyed in this book may be of interest but, so far as they are concerned, not of any real use in the world of today. They consider religion outmoded and look upon conventional religious terms and ideas as expressions of wishful thinking devoid of any reality and validity. To these "humanists" a devotion to social values, to purely human objectives, is enough of a religion. The critic of humanism, on the other hand, contends that such a faith is illusory, for science, ethics, and social values are not enough. A transcendent criterion is lacking and there are no passionate convictions. It is another "quasi-faith."

Most striking of the substitutes for religion have been the doctrines of communism and fascism. In each there were —and are—many of the characteristics of religious movements through the centuries. Each had a yearning for the messianic and so were susceptible to the manipulation of such messiah-like dictators as Lenin, Stalin, Hitler, and Mussolini. Each movement had a reverence for its basic writings and elevated them into "sacred" scriptures (*Das Kapital, Mein Kampf,* etc.). Commissars and *Gauleiters,* no matter how cruel—and indeed perhaps because of their cruelty—formed virtually a priesthood. The rulers and the ruled observed sacred days such as May Day or *Partei Tag* and revered the word of the Leader—the utterances of Red China's Mao Tse-tung, for instance. The political philosophy of the Marxists (called "dialectical materialism") explained the inexorable, inevitable process of the evolution of mankind from the primitive communism of earliest times to the perfect society of the future when "the dictatorship of the proletariat" would cause the state to "wither away"; and it anticipated a kind of "Kingdom of God" with justice and equality in a classless society (". . . from each according to his abilities, to each according to his needs"). The theory is appealing, but in its political and economic manifestations, whether in the Soviet Union and its satellite neighbors or in Red China, Marxism in practice has often substituted greater injustices for the injustice it claimed to be supplanting.

Karl Marx said that religion was "the opiate of the people"; yet the faith of his followers echoes the Hebrew prophets and the early Christians in damning the acquisitive urge and inveighing against accumulation of property. Communists may deny that their beliefs constitute a religion, but denial does not gainsay the fact that their political credo is for them the "center of history." They claim to be atheists, but nevertheless accord to certain ideals and objectives the kind of worship and devotion usually reserved for religion. For many a modern man communism seems to provide a substitute for a more formal, long-established faith; and Marxism affords a seductive philosophy in giving contemporary history both dynamism and drama. The dynamic and dramatic appear in abundance in annals of the past and are strikingly evident in the history of religions, but seem to be lacking in religious institutions and movements today. Communism offers an attractive substitute for people too unsophisticated to perceive that its present-day outlook and achievements are misleading.

From the ferment of ideas and events in the last half of the nineteenth century and the opening decades of the twentieth century, the movement known as "existential-ism" emerged, part of it a non-theistic, avowedly atheistic school of thought (from Nietzsche to Sartre) and the other part theistic (from Kierkegaard to Tillich). Although existentialism has become something of a fad, it has played a very important role in creating much that is valid and significant in the literature, art, and thought since World War II.

Primarily concerned with the mood of modern man and with the terrible choices demanded of all who share human existence today, existentialism puts forth the demand that man be human, not mechanized, not enamored of "progress" and its spurious objectives, not dehumanized or compartmentalized, not unrelated to the truth men try to grasp, not entranced by objectivity or ensnared by rationalism.

The attractiveness of existentialism, the sheer magnetism of its ideas, the power of the movement—whether with an idea of God or without one—derive from its stress on the centrality of man, his aloneness, his reluctant but inevitable commitments, his inescapable freedom as contrasted to his limitations and finiteness. Existentialism, whether anti-theistic or pro-theistic, lays emphasis on sincerity and inwardness, on intuition and involvement. It seeks to protect the individual and his creativity in the midst of a society which creates pressures that inhibit and destroy.

From the existentialist movement came much of the impetus for the "death of God" movement. When Nietzsche declared almost a century ago that God was dead, he was sounding a dirge and celebrating funeral rites at the grave of a conception of God which he had learned in childhood but rejected in adulthood. He was anticipating the "death" of many lesser gods, both false and real, which two World Wars and the threat of a third were ultimately to destroy. This kind of "deicide," this wholesale destruction of inadequate, specious ideas of God, is wholesome, decidedly salutary.

It is this same drive for honesty in thought, for authenticity in commitment, for integrity of the harassed individual that has given such momentum to the "death of God" movement of our time. If to Nietzsche the God of the bourgeoisie in Germany in particular and Europe in general was dead, so for many in our day the God of the middle class of America in particular and of Western civilization in general is dead, dead beyond recall. In ancient days the most meaningful message in religion came from those who first destroyed the idols. No less in our day do men try to discern truth in the midst of illusion and idolatry, such as the vain hope that science will be our salvation, or a belief in the false god of "progress." Only by rejecting such delusions can mankind move on toward a more valid, more vital, meaningful concept of God.

The unmistakable impact of existentialism and the all-pervasive influence of the "death of God" movement have an added importance in the light of the spiritual problems in the last third of the twentieth century, when decisions more difficult than men had ever imagined face this generation. All living religions today—not just Judaism and Christianity, as many Americans mistakenly think—are affected by problems of unprecedented complexity.

The vast changes in the world during recent decades and the extraordinary difficulties faced by three billion people with their myriad tongues and cultures have caused some people to plead for a single world religion as a necessary precondition for the establishment of peace and equity among nations. There will, however, never be a world religion in which all men share a core of basic beliefs, simple as such a solution seems, attractive though it appears. Not only would it be impossible, but a world religion unified in structure and uniform in thought, even if possible, is neither necessary nor desirable.

Religion needs passion and drive to mold the minds of men and lead them, a unique meaning and a specific content to leave a mark on history's pages. Such objectives are not attained by a diluted faith created by wishful thinking, or by a naïve view of a unified, simplified world. The promise of such a world has been dangled before the peoples of many nations by dictators seeking power or justifying their wars in the name of whatever movement was on the rise in that moment in history.

Many young people in the United States in the late 1960s, disillusioned with such quasi-religions as nationalism, fascism, and communism, and opposed to their country's military involvement in Vietnam, have evolved a philosophy of their own. They repudiate war and the values of a generation that countenances war as a solution to problems. "Make love, not war," they advise. These young people also reject the Western religions and turn to religions of the East—especially Hinduism and Buddhism—for spiritual guidance. For them the individual is all-important. In their eyes the real objective is being spared the spiritual death which bigness in industry, labor, and government seems to make inevitable. The flaws in their solution are their withdrawal from society, their refusal to work constructively, their reluctance to remedy these problems creatively, their failure to suggest any better answers than those they might have found in the basic philosophy of the world's living religions.

Men have always faced tragedy and death, tried to seek good and shun evil; they have fought boredom and despair and sought to learn restraint, find courage, cope with catastrophe, fend off disease and destruction. In our time men must do no less; and in our need we, too, turn to the resources of religion.

There is, however, a new spirit animating religious dialogue today. Just as the ecumenical movement is bringing greater unity among the Christian churches, so too philosophers and priests, teachers and writers are in closer touch with one another, sharing their insights with colleagues of other lands and faiths.

The novel aspect of this interaction of faiths in our day is that the interchange is so fruitful. At no time in previous centuries have religious faiths been so near each other as radio, television, worldwide communication by satellite on an instantaneous basis, and the wide circulation of printed matter have brought them. Most of the inhabitants of the world are more aware of other lands and other faiths than their fathers and grandfathers were; inevitably they are also becoming aware that other religions have parallels to their own, as well as valued differences in both belief and practice. Such an awareness will grow, not diminish, in coming years; and in this respect the hundreds of millions who adhere to the major religions cannot help but be influenced toward a greater mutual respect.

Socrates left a priceless legacy in his declaration: "I am neither Athenian nor Greek but a citizen of the world." He presaged the world of twenty-five centuries later in which, whether we are Americans or Europeans, Asiatics or Africans, we are the heirs to the spiritual treasures of every age, of every land.

Suggested Reading

GENERAL SURVEYS

BALLOU, ROBERT O. (ed.). *The Portable World Bible:* A Comprehensive Selection From the Eight Sacred Scriptures of the World. New York: Viking Press, 1944.

BURTT, EDWIN A. *Man Seeks the Divine:* A Study in the History and Comparisons of Religions. New York: Harper & Brothers, 1957.

ELIADE, MIRCEA. *Patterns in Comparative Religion.* New York: Sheed & Ward, 1958.

FINEGAN, JACK. *Archaeology of World Religions.* Princeton, New Jersey: Princeton University Press, 1952.

HUTCHISON, JOHN A., and MARTIN, JAMES A., JR. *Ways of Faith:* An Introduction to Religion. New York: Ronald Press Company, 1960.

NORTHROP, F. S. C. *The Meeting of East and West:* An Inquiry Concerning World Understanding. New York: Macmillan Company, 1946.

173

SCHOEPS, HANS-JOACHIM. *The Religions of Mankind:* Their Origin and Development. Garden City, N.Y.: Doubleday & Company, 1966.

SMITH, HUSTON. *The Religions of Man.* New York: Harper & Brothers, 1958; New American Library of World Literature paperback, 1959.

WATTS, HAROLD H. *The Modern Reader's Guide to Religions.* New York: Barnes & Noble, 1964.

PREHISTORIC AND PRIMITIVE RELIGIONS

FRAZER, JAMES G. *The Golden Bough.* 12 vols. London: Macmillan Company, 1911–15; one vol., abridged edition, New York, 1922, 1951.

HOWELLS, W. M. *The Heathens: Primitive Man and His Religions.* New York: Doubleday & Company, 1948.

JAMES, E. O. *Prehistoric Religion.* New York: Harper & Brothers, 1957.

MOORE, GEORGE FOOT. *The Birth and Growth of Religion.* New York: Charles Scribner's Sons, 1923.

MALINOWSKI, BRONISLAW. *Magic, Science, and Religion.* Boston: Beacon Press, 1948; Doubleday & Company, Anchor paperback, 1954.

RADIN, PAUL. *Primitive Religion: Its Nature and Origin.* New York: Viking Press, 1957; Dover paperback.

BABYLONIAN RELIGION

FRANKFORT, HENRI. *Kingship and the Gods.* Chicago: University of Chicago Press, 1948.

JASTROW, MORRIS. *Aspects of Religious Belief and Practice in Babylonia and Assyria.* New York: G. P. Putnam's Sons, 1911.

LANGDON, S. *Babylonian Epic of Creation.* New York and London: Oxford University Press, 1923.

PRITCHARD, JAMES B. (ed.). *Ancient Near East Texts.* Princeton, New Jersey: Princeton University Press, 1950; rev. 1955.

EGYPTIAN RELIGION

BREASTED, JAMES H. *Development of Religion and Thought in Ancient Egypt*. New York: Charles Scribner's Sons, 1912; Harper & Brothers paperback, 1959.

BUDGE, E. A. WALLIS. *From Fetish to God in Ancient Egypt*. New York and London: Oxford University Press, 1934.

FRANKFORT, HENRI. *Ancient Egyptian Religion*. New York: Columbia University Press, 1949.

PETRIE, W. M. FLINDERS. *Religious Life in Ancient Egypt*. Boston: Houghton Mifflin Company, 1924.

GREEK RELIGION

DURANT, WILL. *The Life of Greece*. Vol. II in *The Story of Civilization;* New York: Simon & Schuster, 1939.

GUTHRIE, W. K. C. *The Greeks and Their Gods*. Boston: Beacon Press, 1950; paperback, 1955.

JAEGER, WERNER. *Paideia: The Ideals of Greek Culture*. New York and London: Oxford University Press, 1943, 1945.

MURRAY, GILBERT. *Five Stages of Greek Religion*. London: Oxford University Press, 1925; Doubleday & Co., Anchor paperback, 1955.

ROMAN RELIGION

ANGUS, SAMUEL. *Religious Quests of the Graeco-Roman World*. New York: Charles Scribner's Sons, 1929.

BAILEY, CYRIL. *Phases of the Religion of Ancient Rome*. Berkeley, California: University of California Press, 1932.

DURANT, WILL. *Caesar and Christ*. Vol. III in *The Story of Civilization*. New York: Simon & Schuster, 1944.

ROSE, H. J. *Ancient Roman Religion*. London: Hutchinson & Company, 1948; combined with *Ancient Greek Religion* (1946) and published in New York by Harper & Brothers as paperback with new title: *Religion in Greece and Rome, 1959.*

HINDUISM

DE BARY, WM. THEODORE; HAY, STEPHEN; WEILER, ROYAL; YARROW, ANDREW. *Sources of Indian Tradition*. Number LVI in *Introduction to Oriental Civilizations*. New York: Columbia University Press, 1958.

LIN YUTANG (ed.). *The Wisdom of China and India*. New York: Random House, 1942.

NIKHILANANDA, SWAMI. *Hinduism: Its Meaning for the Liberation of the Spirit*. New York: Harper & Row, 1958.

RADHAKRISHNAN, SARVEPALLI. *Eastern Religions and Western Thought*. New York: Oxford University Press, 1939; Galaxy paperback, 1959.

SCHWEITZER, ALBERT. *Indian Thought and Its Development*. New York: Henry Holt & Company, 1936; Boston: Beacon Press, 1952; Beacon paperback, 1957.

ZIMMER, HEINRICH (JOSEPH CAMPBELL, ed.). *Philosophies of India*. New York: Bollingen Foundation, 1951; Meridian paperback, 1956.

SIKHISM

ARCHER, JOHN CLARK. *The Sikhs: In Relation to Hindus, Moslems, Christians, and Ahmadiyyas*. Princeton, New Jersey: Princeton University Press, 1946.

GUPTA, H. R. *History of the Sikhs*. London: Dawson Publishers, 1950.

(*See also: Eastern Religions and Western Thought* by Sarvepalli Radhakrishnan, *Indian Thought and Its Development* by Albert Schweitzer, and *Philosophies of India* by Heinrich Zimmer.)

ZOROASTRIANISM

DHALLA, M. N. *History of Zoroastrianism*. London: Oxford University Press, 1938.

HERZFELD, ERNEST. *Zoroaster and His World*. Princeton, New Jersey: Princeton University Press, 1947.

MOULTON, JAMES HOPE. *The Treasure of the Magi*. London: Oxford University Press, 1917.

JAINISM

BUHLER, J. G. *On the Indian Sect of the Jains.* London: Luzac & Company, 1903.

JAIN, J. L. *Outlines of Jainism.* London: Cambridge University Press, 1916, 1940.

PRATT, JAMES BISSETT. *India and Its Faiths.* Boston: Houghton Mifflin Company, 1915.

STEVENSON, MARGARET. *The Heart of Jainism.* New York: Oxford University Press, 1920.

(*See also: Eastern Religions and Western Thought* by Sarvepalli Radhakrishnan, and *Indian Thought and Its Development* by Albert Schweitzer.)

BUDDHISM

BURTT, EDWIN A. (ed.). *The Teachings of the Compassionate Buddha: Early Discourses, The Dhammapada and Later Basic Writings.* New York: New American Library of World Literature, 1955.

CARUS, PAUL. *The Gospel of the Buddha.* Chicago: Open Court Publishers, 1917.

MORGAN, KENNETH (ed.). *The Path of the Buddha.* New York: Ronald Press, 1956.

PRATT, JAMES BISSETT. *The Pilgrimage of Buddhism: And a Buddhist Pilgrimage.* New York: Macmillan Company, 1928.

SCHWEITZER, ALBERT. *Indian Thought and Its Development.* New York: Henry Holt & Company, 1936; Boston: Beacon Press, 1952; paperback, 1957.

ZIMMER, HEINRICH (JOSEPH CAMPBELL, ed.). *Philosophies of India.* New York: Bollingen Foundation, Inc., 1951; Meridian Books, 1956.

ZEN BUDDHISM

BARRETT, WILLIAM. *Zen Buddhism: Selected Writings of D. T. Suzuki.* Garden City, N.Y.: Doubleday & Company, 1956.

KAPLEAU, PHILIP (trans. and ed.). *The Three Pillars of Zen: Teaching, Practice and Enlightenment.* New York: Harper & Row, 1966.

PHILLIPS, BERNARD (ed.). *The Essentials of Zen Buddhism: From Writings of Daisetz Teitaro Suzuki.* New York: E. P. Dutton & Co., 1962.

ROSS, NANCY WILSON (ed.). *The World of Zen: An East-West Anthology.* New York: Random House, 1960.

WATTS, ALAN W. *The Way of Zen.* New York: Pantheon Books, 1957.

CONFUCIANISM

DE BARY, WILLIAM THEODORE (ed.). *Sources of Chinese Tradition.* Number LV in *Introduction to Oriental Civilizations,* New York: Columbia University Press, 1958.

CHAN, WING-TSIT (trans. and comp.). *A Source Book in Chinese Philosophy.* Princeton, New Jersey: Princeton University Press, 1963.

——— . Religious Trends in Modern China. New York: Columbia University Press, 1953.

CREEL, H. G. *Chinese Thought: From Confucius to Mao Tse-tung.* Chicago: University of Chicago Press, 1953.

LIN YUTANG (trans.). *The Wisdom of Confucius.* New York: Modern Library, 1938.

WARE, JAMES (trans. and comp.). *The Sayings of Mencius.* New York: New American Library of World Literature, 1960.

TAOISM

BLAKNEY, R. B. (trans. and ed.). *The Way of Life: Lao Tzu.* New York: New American Library of World Literature, 1955.

CHAN, WING-TSIT (trans. and ed.). *The Wisdom of Laotse.* New York: Modern Library, 1948.

MAURER, HERRYMON. *The Old Fellow.* New York: John Day Company, 1943.

WALEY, ARTHUR. *The Way and Its Power: A Study of the Tao Te Ching and Its Place in Chinese Thought*. New York: Macmillan Company, 1934.

WELCH, HOLMES. *The Parting of the Ways: Lao Tzu and the Taoist Movement*. Boston: Beacon Press, 1957.

SHINTO

ANESAKI, MASAHARU. *History of Japanese Religions: With Special Reference to the Social and Moral Life of the Nation*. Rutland, Vermont, and Tokyo, Japan: Charles E. Tuttle Company, 1963.

HOLTOM, D. C. *Modern Japan and Shinto Nationalism*. Chicago: University of Chicago Press, 1943 and 1947.

HOLTOM, D. C. *The National Faith of Japan*. New York: E. P. Dutton & Co., 1938.

McFARLAND, H. NEILL. *The Rush Hour of the Gods: A Study of New Religious Movements in Japan*. New York: Macmillan Company, 1967.

THOMSEN, HARRY. *The New Religions of Japan*. Rutland, Vermont, and Tokyo, Japan: Charles E. Tuttle Company, 1963.

TSUNODA, RYUSAKU; DE BARY, WM. THEODORE; KEENE, DONALD (eds.). *Sources of the Japanese Tradition*. Number LIV in *Introduction to Oriental Civilizations*. New York: Columbia University Press, 1958.

JUDAISM

BAECK, LEO. (ALBERT H. FRIEDLANDER, trans.). *This People Israel: The Meaning of Jewish Existence*. Philadelphia: Jewish Publication Society of America, 1965.

DAVIS, MOSHE. *The Emergence of Conservative Judaism: The Historical School in 19th Century America*. Philadelphia: Jewish Publication Society of America, 1963.

GLATZER, NAHUM N. (ed.). *Texts in the Judaic Tradition*. Vol. I, *The Rest Is Commentary: A Source Book of Judaic Antiquity;* Vol. II, *Faith and Knowledge: The Jew in the Medieval World;* Vol. III, *The Dynamics of Emancipation: The Jew in the Modern World*. Boston: Beacon Press, 1961.

GRAYZEL, SOLOMON. *A History of the Jews: From the Babylonian Exile to the Establishment of Israel.* Philadelphia: Jewish Publication Society of America, 1947.

PARKES, JAMES. *A History of the Jewish People.* Baltimore, Maryland: Penguin Books, 1964.

PLAUT, W. GUNTHER. *The Rise of Reform Judaism: A Sourcebook of Its European Origins.* New York: World Union for Progressive Judaism, Ltd., 1963.

CHRISTIANITY

ADAM, KARL. *The Spirit of Catholicism.* New York: Macmillan Company, 1940. Doubleday & Co., paperback, 1959.

BAINTON, ROLAND H. *Christendom: A Short History of Christianity and Its Impact on Western Civilization.* (Published as *The Horizon History of Christianity.*) New York: American Heritage Publishing Co., 1964. New York: Harper & Row, 1966.

BROWN, ROBERT MCAFEE. *The Spirit of Protestantism.* New York: Oxford University Press, 1961.

HERBERG, WILL. *Protestant–Catholic–Jew: An Essay in American Religious Sociology.* Garden City, New York: Doubleday & Co., 1955, 1960.

LATOURETTE, KENNETH SCOTT. *A History of Christianity.* New York: Harper & Row, 1953.

WALKER, WILLISTON. *The History of the Christian Church* (revised by Cyril C. Richardson, Wilhelm Pauck, and Robert T. Handy). New York: Charles Scribner's Sons, 1959.

ISLAM

PAYNE, ROBERT. *The Holy Sword: The Story of Islam from Muhammad to the Present.* New York: Harper & Row, 1959.

RAHMAN, FAZLER. *Islam.* New York: Holt, Rinehart & Winston, 1966.

SMITH, WILFRED CANTWELL. *Islam in Modern History.* Princeton, New Jersey: Princeton University Press, 1957; New American Library of World Literature, 1959.

Von Grunebaum, Gustave E. *Islam: Essays in the Nature and Growth of a Cultural Tradition*. New York: Barnes & Noble, 1961.

———. *Medieval Islam: A Study in Cultural Orientation*. Chicago and London: University of Chicago Press, 1946, 1954; Phoenix Books paperback, 1961.

———. *Modern Islam: The Search for Cultural Identity*. Los Angeles: University of California Press, 1962; New York: Alfred A. Knopf, Vintage Books, paperback, 1964.

BAHAI

Gaver, Jessyca Russell. *The Baha'i Faith*. New York: Hawthorn Books, 1967.

Townshend, George (ed.). *The Glad Tidings of Baha'u'llah: Being Extracts from the Sacred Writings of the Baha'is*. London: John Murray, 1949.

EXISTENTIALISM

Barrett, William. *What Is Existentialism?* New York: Grove Press, Inc., 1964.

Blackham, H. J. *Six Existentialist Thinkers*. New York: Harper & Row, 1959.

Herberg, Will. *Four Existentialist Theologians*. Garden City, New York: Doubleday & Co., 1958.

Kierkegaard, Søren. *Either/Or*. Garden City, New York: Doubleday & Co., 1959.

Shinn, Roger L. *Existentialist Posture*. New York, Association Press, 1959.

Wild, John. *Challenge of Existentialism*. Bloomington, Indiana: Indiana University Press, 1955.

NON-THEISTIC HUMANISM

Dewey, John. *A Common Faith*. New Haven: Yale University Press, 1934.

Frankel, Charles. *The Case for Modern Man*. New York: Harper & Row, 1956.

HAYDON, A. EUSTACE. *Biography of the Gods*. New York: Macmillan Company, 1942.

LAMONT, CORLISS. *The Philosophy of Humanism*. New York: Frederick Ungar Publishing Co., 1965.

MASLOW, ABRAHAM H. *Religion, Values and Peak-Experiences*. Columbus, Ohio: Ohio State University Press, 1964.

PATTON, KENNETH. *Religion for One World*. Boston: Beacon Press, 1964.

Acknowledgments

The author and The World Publishing Company wish to thank the following authors and publishers for permission to quote from the books listed. All possible care has been taken to ensure accuracy; however, if any errors have accidentally occurred, they will be corrected in subsequent editions provided notification is sent to the publisher.

EDWARD ARNOLD & Co., London: *Hinduism and Buddhism,* by Sir Charles Eliot, vol. 3, 1921.

ASSOCIATION PRESS, New York: *Gotama Buddha: A Biography Based on the Canonical Books of the Theravadin,* by Kenneth Saunders, 1920.

BEACON PRESS, Boston: *The Rest Is Commentary,* by Nahum N. Glatzer, 1961.

CONSTABLE & Co., LTD., London: *Early Zoroastrianism,* by James Hope Moulton, 1913.

J. M. DENT & SONS LTD., and E. P. DUTTON & Co., New York: *The Koran,* translated by J. M. Rodwell, 1909.

Hind Kitabs Ltd., Bombay: *Great Indians,* by S. Radhakrishnan, 1949.

Jewish Publication Society of America, Philadelphia: *The Holy Scriptures,* 1917, 1945.

David McKay Company, Inc., New York: *The Story of Confucius,* by Brian Brown, 1927.

The Macmillan Company, New York: *This Believing World,* by Lewis Browne, 1926.

John Murray, London: *Buddhist Scriptures,* translated by Edward J. Thomas; *The Sayings of Confucius,* translated and edited by Lionel Giles; *The Conduct of Life,* a translation by Ku Hung Ming of *The Doctrine of the Mean; The Saying of Lao Tzu,* translated by Lionel Giles; selections from *Wisdom of the East,* 1905, 1906, 1913, 1917.

Oxford University Press, London: *Sacred Books of the East,* by F. Max Mueller (ed.), vol. 22, translated by Hermann Jacobi, 1884.

Pali Text Society, London: *Further Dialogues of the Buddha,* translated from the *Majjhima Nikaya,* by Lord Chalmers, vol. 1, 1926.

Charles Scribner's Sons, New York: *Poems,* by George Santayana, 1923, 1951.

Vedanta Society of Southern California, Hollywood, Calif.: *Bhagavad-Gita: The Song of God,* translated by Swami Prabhavananda and Christopher Isherwood, 1950.

The Viking Press, Inc., New York: *The Analects of Confucius,* translated by Charles A. Wong, reprinted in *The Bible of The World,* edited by Robert O. Ballou.

Index

ABOUT THE AUTHOR

CARL HERMANN VOSS has held pastorates in Raleigh, N.C., Pittsburgh, Pa., Brooklyn, N.Y., and Saratoga Springs, N.Y., has served as an executive of international church organizations in New York City, and has taught at the New School for Social Research, Skidmore College, and the Theological School of St. Lawrence University. He received the degrees of Bachelor of Arts and Doctor of Philosophy from the University of Pittsburgh; and after study abroad, he earned his Bachelor of Divinity degree at Union Theological Seminary in New York City. His other books include *The Universal God, The Palestine Problem Today,* and *Rabbi and Minister.* He is editor of Excalibur Books.

2   3   4   5   72   71   70   69

FLORA PUBLIC LIBRARY
Madison County Library System

1-14-01